*Tempus* ORAL HISTORY *Series*

# *voices of*
# Ashton-under-Lyne

Evelyn Kington, actress stepmother of the *Three Little Girls Together*, as Sousa in *A Chinese Honeymoon*.

*Ashton Market on a busy day in the 1950s .*

*Tempus* ORAL HISTORY *Series*

# *voices of*
# Ashton-under-Lyne

*Compiled by*
Derek J. Southall

TEMPUS

First published 2000
Copyright © Derek J. Southall, 2000

Tempus Publishing Limited
The Mill, Brimscombe Port,
Stroud, Gloucestershire, GL5 2QG

ISBN 0 7524 2160 3

Typesetting and origination by
Tempus Publishing Limited
Printed in Great Britain by
Midway Clark Printing, Wiltshire

For David and Gill and my grandchildren, Steven and Melissa

Front cover: *The Redford Family in the Dingle, a popular part of Stamford Park, c. 1910.*

*Queen's Road Methodist church Boy's Brigade, c. 1931.*

# Contents

*Ryecroft Congregational Church Girl Guides in 1928. The minister is Mr Wheatcroft.*

# Introduction

When I was asked by my publisher, early in 1999, to compile a book called *Voices of Ashton-under-Lyne*, my initial reaction was to say, 'I couldn't do that. For a start, I wasn't born in Ashton-under-Lyne, and, secondly, I've only lived here for forty years'. Convinced by the publisher that it was a task which I could undertake, I embarked on the enterprise and here, eighteen months on, is the finished book.

    *Voices of Ashton-under-Lyne* falls into the category of what is termed 'Oral History', and it is important to recognize the way in which oral history differs from our general interpretation of history. When we speak of history, we usually mean carefully researched historical facts, backed up by tangible evidence. Oral history, however, although it too deals in facts, does not have its foundation in careful research. Rather it is the recorded memories of people who lived through an era and who are able to recall that era for the reader through their recorded memories. Memory, as we all are only too well aware, is not always as reliable as we would like it to be. While the gist of an incident, or a well-known event, or a personal experience is easy enough to recall, specific facts related to those things may not be as easily recollected, or may be recollected imperfectly. So, if what you're looking for is accurate historical fact, oral history is not the place to find it. If, on the other hand, what you want is to know what it was like to live in a particular place in a particular era, as remembered by people who lived in that place in that era, then oral history is for you. In it you will find the joys, the sadness, the high and low

*Albion School and Sunday School at top of Penny Meadow, from Fraser Street.*

spots, family events and town events seen through the eyes of the people whose memories are recorded. You will also see, with their eyes, the streets and buildings – some long vanished – of the town in which they lived, and of which they often speak with much affection.

This oral history of Ashton-under-Lyne during the first half of the twentieth century is an attempt to create a picture of life in this industrial town (lying some seven miles to the East of Manchester) from the recollections of people who were born there in the first thirty years or so of that century. At that time Ashton was part of Lancashire; since then, since 1972 to be precise, it has been part of the Metropolitan Borough of Tameside and of Greater Manchester.

The book has been put together from tape-recorded interviews which I conducted, over a period of fifteen months, with nearly thirty people who were born in Ashton in the first half of the last century. Many of them have lived in the town all their lives: one remarkable lady for almost a century. In order to interview them I visited them in their homes, where I was, on every occasion, warmly welcomed. Once I had the tape-recorded interviews, I transcribed each one; then, from the transcriptions, I selected those parts of the interviews which I felt fitted my purpose most effectively; it is those which I have used to compile my book. I would like to record here that conducting the interviews was a most pleasurable job. The people I interviewed spoke freely, and what they had to say was, invariably, quite fascinating. Indeed, it was sometimes only the fact that the 90-minute tape ran out that brought an interview to its conclusion. I'd like to thank them all for welcoming me into their homes and for their willingness to talk about their lives, and to share with me, and ultimately with a much wider audience, their memories, even those which were sad, and sometimes painful.

The memories of the Ashton people which make up this book are illustrated by many photographs. A large number of these were loaned to me by the inteviewees, who have kindly given me permission to use them in the book. The photographs, often of family members, were invaluable in giving the book the personal touch that oral history needs to make it come alive. I am most grateful to everyone who loaned me their photographs; I know how precious they are, and how much you treasure them.

It is my hope that the picture of life in Ashton-under-Lyne which is created in these pages is a true reflection of the time to which it relates as well as being an accurate transcription of what was told to me. I have tried throughout to use only the words used by those whom I interviewed, believing that it is vitally important to be true to what they said. A word or two – in square brackets – has occasionally been inserted by me for the sake of clarity.

If I may, I will close this introduction on a personal note. My wife and I were both born and brought up in a small town at the head of one of the South Wales mining valleys. I moved to the North-West when I started my teaching career and my wife joined me when we married. We have lived in Ashton now for more than forty years, and we both regard it as home. It is my hope that *Voices of Ashton-under-Lyne* is a fitting tribute to our 'home' town.

# Acknowledgements

I would like to record my thanks to those whose words and photographs make up this book for the unstinting and generous way in which they responded to my requests for interviews and pictures. The initials of its contributor are at the end of each block of text. They are: Mrs Annie Armitage (A.A.); Mrs Ada Brown (Mrs A.B.); Mr Alan Brown (A.B.); Mrs Elsie Brown (E.B.); Mrs Margaret Booth (M.B.); Mr Norman Buckley (N.B.); Mr Ernest Copeland (E.C.); Mrs Elizabeth Copeland (Mrs E.C.); Mr Harold Craig (H.C.); Mr Jack Evans (J.E.); Mr David Fletcher (D.F.); Miss Hilda Fielding (H.F.); Mrs Alice Greenwood (A.G.); Mr Frank Harrison (F.H.); Mrs Ida Holland (I.H.); Mr Harry Iliffe (H.I.); Mrs Joyce Iliffe (J.I.); Mr David Jones (D.J.); Mr Hubert King (H.K.); Mrs Mattie Lee (M.L.); Mrs Ellen Murphy (E.M.); Mr Jack Millin (J.M.); Mr Brian Noke (B.N.); Mr Bob Parkinson (B.P.); Mr Frank Ruffley (F.R.); Mr Albert Shaw (A.S.); Mrs Dorothy Sidebottom (D.S.); Mrs Ivy Shawcross (I.S.); Miss Grace Wardle (G.W.); Mrs May Worrall (M.W.).

My sincere thanks also to Alice Lock and the staff of the Local Studies Library at Stalybridge for their patience and the invaluable help which they gave me in my efforts to find some of the photographs which are included in the book and for permission to reproduce them.

The picture of the van with the John Hill's Biscuits logo is reproduced by permission of Castle and Fielding Ltd. Body-builders, Ashton-under-Lyne. Thanks to Mr and Mrs D. Bolt for the cover picture.

My thanks to my wife for her constant encouragement and patience during the many months which it has taken me to complete the book.

# CHAPTER 1
## Childhood Memories

*'Three Little Girls Together' – Alice, Margaret and Mary Wood.*

### Fish and Teacakes

My grandfather had a fish shop and my uncle used to go round with a horse and cart, selling fish. When we moved from Broadbent Avenue onto Smallshaw Lane, all the furniture went round on that horse and cart. My sister and I used to go on our bicycles round Higher Hurst on a Friday night and collect fish orders and take them back to Granddad. He used to make them up early on Saturday morning. We used to go across and, on our bikes, we used to go round and deliver the fish. Grandma made teacakes and she used to sell them to people. We used to deliver those as well.

(H.F.)

*Margaret Street, where Joyce and Grace Wardle asked, 'Can we do your step?'*

## Three Little Girls Together

My mother died when I was five. We went to live with Grandpa. When Grandpa died, we really, for two years, looked after each other. Alice and I had a sister, Mary, then. She died when she was twenty-three of rheumatic fever. We went to Trafalgar School and Trafalgar Sunday School, three times every Sunday. We were always late, the three of us, because we had jobs to do.

(M.B.)

## Can I Do Your Step?

Being little girls, we used to go up the street sandstoning people's doorsteps – 'Can I do your step?' Sometimes they would give us a penny, but my mother didn't like us taking anything off anyone, so we had to say, 'No, thank you'.

(J.I.)

## Clay Pies and Cleaning Windows

We used to go out in the back and make clay pies. Then you used to open up the shop – 'Come and Buy' – and you used to buy those clay pies, that you'd made, with buttons. And you'd run in for a bread and butter and you'd get a big thick piece of home-made bread with jam on it; you'd call in the toilet on your way out, eating your bread and jam. All this cleanliness

10

today hasn't done anyone any good. I remember we used to have to sit on the bedroom window sills to clean the windows. We used to put the window up, sit on the window sill, pull the window down across our lap, clean the window, then do the other one. Then you stoned your window sill. Then you did your bedrooms. Washed all the lino. We used to spread tea-leaves on the carpet and then brush it. When my father married my step-mother, who was an actress, we did all the work.

(M.B.)

## Taking a Pig to Oldham

Lees Road, the road to Oldham, although it was straight, wasn't a road. Y'had boulders sticking up out of it. When me father was a farm labourer, we used to take a pig to a butcher in Oldham for slaughter. We went along Lees Road and it was an eventful journey. I used to go, because the butcher always gave me a pork pie.

(H.C.)

## Wash Day

I remember washing used to take a full day. If she was doing blankets or something of that sort, my mother used to send me down the ginnel to Mrs Lomas at Number 56 to see if we could borrow her lines. The old set boiler in the corner, the dolly tub, the rubbing board – washing used to take all day, and it involved all of us.

(A.B.)

## The Milk Round

When my father was a farm labourer, he drove the horse for the milk round. The horse knew where to stop. It was amazing. I was up there at the farm once and Mr Gledhill said, 'You'll have to take the milk round today'. I said, 'I don't know where to go'. 'Th' horse does', he said. Everywhere the horse stopped, I went there and that was it. You had a churn, and you had small measures like a ladle, and the milk was doled into the receptacle which the people had.

(H.C.)

Alan Brown's mum and dad outside 62 Cambridge Street.

*The entrance to Stamford Park.*

## Day Out in Stamford Park

As a treat from church we used to have tickets given to us and we used to come up to Stamford Park. That was wonderful, for us to come to Stamford Park when we were kids. We would have a badge on, and they'd give us a ticket, and we'd have a free ride on the steamer. We had an ice-cream and we had a little tea in the refreshment room. There was no playground then.

(A.G.)

## Legging Tunnel

We were poor. Well, the good people of Ashton had a fund, to give the poor children of Ashton a treat. I remember quite clearly going on the 'Poor Children's Treat'. This was a ride to Marple on the canal, on a coal barge, a horse pulling. It was like a

holiday, really, for us who'd never been anywhere. I always remember Legging Tunnel. There's a tunnel just before you come into Marple where there's no towpath. What used to happen then - the bargeman used to lie on top of the cabin and leg the barge through. That's why it's called Legging Tunnel. I remember that, and we had tea in the school just in Marple there. The coal barge, they got some white sheets, y'know - being a cotton place there were plenty of white sheets - to put over it so you didn't get too dirty.

(D.J.)

## Our Willoughby

I remember one incident during the First World War. My mother used to have us all dressed nice. One day she says, 'I'll take you up to Stamford Park; we'll have a picnic'. It

*Stamford Park boating lake with steamer. The building in the background is the refreshment room.*

*The Redford family in the Dingle, a popular part of Stamford Park, c. 1910.*

were a big thing, all going out together with me mum. We were all dressed lovely, white socks and everything. She even used to scrub our nails for us. We had to sit on the two seats at the back of the tram. Me and our mother and our Violet sat at this side, and our John and Tom and Willoughby sat at that side. Our Tom put his foot up and caught our Willoughby's white sock. 'Dirty bugger', our Willoughby says to our Tom. My mother, she says, 'What did you say?' Willoughby says, 'He's a dirty bugger. Look what he's done'. Next stop we were all off, the lot of us. Me mother says, 'Come on, we're going right home, and we're walking it'. She got home and she gave our Willoughby a good hiding. 'Where have you heard that?'. One of his little pals had said it, and he didn't know, did he, bless him! He gets shoved upstairs – this is when we lived on Delamere Street North. Me grandma came round at night and she says, 'Where's the lad?' (She always called him 'the lad', with being the youngest). Me mother says, 'Where is he? I got 'em all dressed up to take 'em to Stamford Park; made a picnic to take 'em to Stamford Park. Did he show me up?' 'The lad showed you up?', me Gran says. 'Oh, yes', she says, 'I'll say he showed me up'. 'How long has he been upstairs?' 'He's been upstairs ever since we came home'. She goes to the bottom of the stairs, me grandma, and she shouts, 'Have you been a naughty boy?' 'Yes', says our Willoughby, 'but if me mummy'll let me come down, I won't swear again, will I buggery'. He didn't know, bless him. He wondered why his mum had smacked him. Me grandma said, 'Poor little thing; he doesn't know he's swearing'. That were me mother; she were very strict. But me dad never hit any of us.

(M.W.)

## Horse and Cart to Manchester

## Market

Me father was a market trader. He was a greengrocer. He used to work for his father, and when his father died, me dad and his brother kept up the stall on the market. Before the war he had a horse and cart. He used to get his stuff from Manchester markets very early in the morning and sometimes he would take me down on his cart. I always had to keep my feet on the bottom of the cart; he wouldn't let me hang me legs over the side. That was quite good fun.

(E.B.)

## The End of the World

My father had been born in Glossop and had come to live in Ashton when he was very young. As children, we used to go up to Glossop on the train and, of course, the railway line ended there. We walked up to his aunt's house and they took us for a walk up to the bottom of the Snake Pass. I thought that was the end of the world. That was as far as I ever went and, I thought, as far as all the traffic went. Of course, there wouldn't be much traffic going over the roads then.

(H.F.)

## Playing Games Outside

I lived on Raynham Street, just off Whiteacre Road. All the children used to be outside. We had a little green opposite where we lived and we used to play out there all day long, especially on school holidays. It never seemed to rain. Then they started to build down Beaufort Road and we used to go down there. We were down there at nine o'clock in the morning. We used to play all sorts of games and, when people had been cutting their lawns and they'd thrown all the cuttings away, we used to throw them at each other. We used to play at shop, with clay, and chop stones up. We used to get through the day without any bother, no falling out or anything.

(Mrs A.B.)

## Dobbers and Jacks

The jacks are four pieces of pottery, really, and they are grooved. Then you get a stone dobber, only like a marble, a biggish marble, and as you threw it you picked a jack up, and as you threw it again, you picked another jack up.

(M.W.)

## My Most Vivid Memory

I think the most vivid memories are playing out with the other children. I remember that – I suppose I was about eight at the time – they built some council houses on Pelham Street, and they put in a macadam road. That road was a great joy to us children; we were able to play whip'n top, y'know. Our childhood seemed to be made up of lovely days when we could play out. I do remember that there were a lot of pieces of spare ground where children could play. I believe that, at the time, when builders built a row of houses, they always stopped the row short, and they didn't have to pay frontage on two streets. So

we used to have lots of places to play.

(I.S.)

## Paper Bombs

We used to make paper bombs as well, that used to hold water, by the same method of folding as you did a paper aeroplane. You'd fill the bomb with water and throw it.

(J.M.)

## Rally Ho!

When we got to Hilton Crescent we used to play all sorts of games there. There used to be a lamp post, which everybody swung on, at the corner of the street. There must have been about ten of us, ten lads who used to knock about with each other. We'd play the usual sort of games – 'Rally Ho!' and 'Kick Can'. 'Rally Ho!', you might have six or seven of you, and one lad would stand under the lamp, where he could see everything. The other kids would hide in somebody's door or behind the trees. If he saw you, he'd shout, 'Rally Ho! One, two, three'. You'd have to rush back to the lamp and he followed you. If he got there before you, it was all right; it was back out again. 'Kick Can' was the same thing; he used to dash back and he'd have to kick the can over before you did.

(B.P.)

## The Button Game

Sometimes we'd pin a button on a window frame or on a door, activated by a string.

People would hear this tapping on the window or door and come; we were a block away then, of course. If a pedestrian came along and got entangled in the string, there was all hell to pay.

(A.B.)

## Onions and Skipping Ropes

We used to wait for the onions to come in at the greengrocer's They were tied up with rope, straw rope. We'd rush to see if we could have that as a skipping rope. 'Can we have the skipping rope off the onions, please?' The onions were in wooden boxes and the rope went round the boxes.

(M.B.)

## The Farmer Wants a Wife

We used to play 'The farmer wants a wife'. You all stood in a ring and picked one person to go in the middle, who was the farmer. Then he picked someone to be a wife; then 'the wife wants a child', 'the child wants a dog', 'the dog wants a bone'. Then everybody shouted, 'They all pat the bone', and everybody patted the bone. Then the bone was the farmer and they all started again.

(G.W.)

## What's That Down There?

My brothers used to get a purse and tie black cotton or something on it. They put it on the pavement and, if somebody bent down to pick it up, they winded the cotton up. We didn't do that, in case somebody caught us and gave us a good hiding.

(M.W.)

## The Youngest Member of the Gang

There used to be gangs and I was always the youngest by about three years. We all played out – there was no television or anything like that – and then it got dark, and I was always the first one to be called in to go to bed, which you don't accept when you're that age – 'Why aren't the others going in?'

(D.F.)

## On Mason's Swings

We used to spend a lot of time playing in the swing park. That belonged to Masons. They were very strict – they sent you out if they found you in the boy's part. They were very serious about boys and girls playing in each other's part. Nobody was allowed in except children around Oxford. The park belonged to the mill.

(D.S.)

## My First Bike

My father was a cyclist, so we all had bicycles. My sister had a bike and they promised to buy me a bike if I passed my scholarship. My sister went to school on hers and I could go on mine. The day I passed my scholarship we looked in the local

*Broadoak Acorns Cycle Speedway Team. Brian Noke is on the extreme right.*

paper and found a bike for sale, for £1, on Lees Road. So my father and I rushed round and the bike was still there. We bought this bike for £1. Dad was very good at doing things up, so it got done up and painted, and that was my first bike for school.

(H.F.)

## Bogies and Bikes

We made our own enjoyment. We used to have what we called 'bogies', made out of pram wheels and a bit of wood. You were posh if you had one with four wheels on; I only ever had one with three wheels on. I had one with one wheel on the front, and we used to push the poker through to steer

it. We went down King's Road, then Hillgate or Union Road. Then, after the war, we started going to Belle Vue, us lads. We made our push-bikes like speedway bikes. There was a league in Manchester, a proper league. We had a team; we were called the 'Broadoak Acorns'.

(B.N.)

## Birds' Eggs and Loco Numbers

I suppose me parents were strict when I think of today's standards. I did have to go to bed early quite a few times, when I'd disappeared over Ashton Moss collecting birds' eggs and it was raining. I'd come home absolutely drenched to the skin. Like a lot of kids I used to watch steam locos. We used to go over to Guide Bridge. Inside Guide Bridge station there's a long footbridge; it was our delight to stand there and wait for locos to come underneath, and get covered in smoke as they went past. Then I'd get home as black as the ace of spades and I'd get a good telling off.

(J.E.)

## Quick Profit

I can remember the trams running from Ashton to Hathershaw. We used to put halfpennies on the tram lane and they'd come out as pennies.

(E.C.)

## My Favourite Toy

I went to school when I was three and a half or four. Can't remember much about it, except that I had an operation when I was four. I can vaguely remember going to school with a bandage round my neck and over my head – the operation was on my neck. I insisted on going back to school before I had the bandages removed. I think it was because I wanted to show off a bit really, and get a bit of fuss. I also remember that I had one of those things – I don't know what you call them – that you blew down. It was like a musical thing; you blew down it and you sang down it and it came out like a tune through a little hole at the top with netting over it. I remember I insisted on taking that back to school with me. I think that perhaps I was a bit of a nuisance really, because they didn't like to tell me I

shouldn't be playing with it. This obviously was my favourite toy.

(H.F.)

## Wood for the Bonfire

At the end of the war we all went mad because fireworks came back in the shops. We used to hear word that some paper shop somewhere had got their fireworks in and we'd go queuing for about an hour and a half to get some fireworks. Then we'd be going round trying to get wood and, like one or two more bad lads at the time, we used to go to other people's bonfires and, when they weren't looking, we used to nick their wood. We'd put a guard on ours then, so that they wouldn't hit back. We had a kind of shift service where we'd keep an eye on the bonfire.

(J.E.)

## I'd Sooner Have a Doll

When I were four years and eight months old, a lady come to our house and she said, 'Nellie, I'm taking you to my chip shop and, when you come back, you'll have a baby'. 'Oh', I said 'I'd sooner have a doll'. She took me to her chip shop and at tea-time she brought me home. She says, 'Come on now. I'm going to show you your baby'. She took me upstairs and there were me little brother. Eh, he did look a funny little thing. And I says, 'When can I take him in t' street and play with him?' My mother, she had my brother and after a fortnight she were back in t'mill. Y'had to be; there was no money. Well I minded him. After he got about two and a half she couldn't afford to pay minder. So I minded my brother from then on. I had a piece of string and a key. I used to put it round his neck. I used to say, 'Sit on our step and just play', and I left him with a ball, while I went to school.

(E.M.)

## Clogs

I had a pair of boots. When I'd worn the bottoms off, me mother had 'em clogged. They had a wooden sole on, and they had metal irons on, like a horseshoe, shaped to the sole. When you run down the street and kicked, you'd get sparks. During the war you couldn't get these metal irons, so they replaced them with rubber underneath. Well, you couldn't get sparks off them then. People used to have best clogs as well. They used to have a pair of clogs for Sunday, some people. Come winter, when it used t'snow, you'd get cloggy bottoms. You'd be a foot taller; the snow used to stick to the clogs. Same with horses; when there were horses on the road, coal horses, the drivers had to keep stopping to knock the snow off, because it built up on the horses' feet.

(B.N.)

## Clog Time

I remember the mills working. Nook Lane, six o'clock in the morning, resounded with clogs, iron clogs; lunchtime again; then at nighttime; you could set the time by the clogs. I think it was about six o'clock at night when they finished.

(H.C.)

## Life on Newmarket Road

Everybody knew each other on Newmarket Road. I couldn't walk down that road without word getting back to my parents that some misdemeanour had been committed. You could short cut down the backs of the houses each side, so you didn't have to walk down the street. We never had our back door locked. The only day we locked our doors and locked our entry doors was Good Friday because we were invaded by people from all over the area to go to Daisy Nook Fair.

(J.M.)

## The Witch Lady and Mammy Miller

Riley Street had maybe fourteen houses. The woman at the end house was into herbs. Of course, when you went into her house, you could always smell them. It was a queer smell. We thought she was a witch, because it was different. But there again, if you ailed anything, that's where you went. She didn't grow the herbs, because we had no gardens or anything like that; she went in the hedgerows. I can see her now – a very big woman she was. And there was a woman called Mrs Miller. That's where we went when we came home from school. We referred to her as Mammy Miller, not Mrs Miller, because she looked after us. Some days she baked, and you'd be in that house and you'd come out with a muffin with jam on it; you didn't have butter, just jam.

(H.C.)

## Sunday Tea at Grandma's

We always went for tea at Grandmother Millin's. These were family get-togethers with the grandparents and the aunts and uncles used to come. We used to be taught to make 'cat's cradles' and things with string and how to do all sorts of tricks. I had this uncle who was a hand-loom weaver. He used to say, 'Is that thick, Jack?', and he used to pinch me to see how thick it was – which I do to the grandchildren now. Grandfather Millin, when he'd done the Sunday cleaning-out of his hens, would then change. 'I'll have a wash'. He'd have a wash, and he'd have his clean union shirt on, and a shirt front, and he'd put a tie and collar on. That was official Sunday then, with high tea – all sorts of things, pressed meat, cowheel pie and everything. My Uncle Harry used to come and my Uncle Lewis and bring their children and there was some extreme politics there. Grandpa Millin was a Tory; his eldest son was a Communist. I used to listen with fascination to their arguments; they'd all read the Sunday paper and put the world to rights.

(J.M.)

## What's Politics?

Mr Potts at butcher's, at corner of Oldham Road and Langham Street there, he were a big member of the Tory club. I remember he got us a couple of tickets for this Christmas party, for me and my youngest brother, Fred. I still remember when we came home with an apple and orange from Tory club – out of bounds otherwise in them days because me family were liberals.

(N.B.)

## A Sunday Stroll

On Sunday we went to Sunday school; mum was a Sunday school teacher. We went to Albion Sunday school at the top of Penny Meadow. We used to sometimes go and have lunch at my grandma's, 'cos she lived on Whiteacre Road. My father used to meet us from Sunday School on a Sunday afternoon and we would walk down to Park Parade, where the bypass is now, and we'd get on the canal bank and then we'd walk right along the canal bank down to the back of Trafalgar Square, because my other grandma lived on Oxford Street, behind the Twelve Apostles. We did this more or less every Sunday. Then we used to have to walk home in the evening. It was quite a hefty walk for children.

(H.F.)

## Half for God!

We were given tuppence to put in the collection at Sunday School, but, more often than not, I stopped off and got two ounces of toffee and put a penny in the collection.

(M.B.)

## Big Days

I remember having a bath on the floor in a big tin bath and having to carry it – three or four of us – through the kitchen and pour it away into the drains. Another big day was when Charlie Lowe came, the chimney sweep. I remember the chimneys being swept and dust everywhere and soot.

Sundays were great days because, among other things, the ice-cream man came round. Then the neighbours would all compete, as soon as the horse and cart went, to scrape up the manure. They used to come out with their buckets and spades Sunday morning – they were all behind the front door, I think – and gather up the manure.

(A.B.)

## The Street Vendors

There was a person who used to come round selling black peas. They had like a push cart, with charcoal in or something, because the peas were hot when you got them. You went out and for a penny you got a bowl of black peas. There was also a person who came round with the contraption with the grindstone on to sharpen knives and scissors and that kind of thing. In those days you used to have a lot of gypsies. They would be selling clothes pegs and that kind of thing.

(H.C.)

## Who Forgot, Then?

As we got a bit older and a bit more adventurous, and perhaps as more traffic came, we had to go over to Jowett's Walk – where the police station is now – to play cricket. We were playing cricket on there, me brother and I and the other lads, and me mother came up, all steaming and excited and shouting her head off.

We'd promised to blow the organ at Henry Square for a wedding which had already started. She took us right from the cricket match to Henry Square church, huffing and puffing, to blow the organ.

(A.B.)

## Broken Melody

I remember the first radio we had. It was a Cossor – the People's set. We bought it from a chap called Hartley, on Penny Meadow. I was always interested in electronics. I remember being in on me own once and I took the back off the radio to see what it was all about. There's an old valve with the top cap on. I thought, 'What's that thing?' Unfortunately it came apart in my hand.

Alan Brown's mum.

21

'I'm in trouble now!' Of course, when they switched it on, it wouldn't work. When the chap came to repair it, he's fiddling about and I said, 'I'll tell you what's wrong with that', and my mother looked at me.

(H.C.)

## Chocolate Drops at Christmas

Chocolate drops were our favourites at Christmas. We had a pound of chocolate drops each. We were allowed to take these with us if we went off to somebody else's house. They were always in different containers. One year they were in a big box with a tassle on top, and you opened it and they were in little compartments. There'd be a quarter pound in a little compartment. Then another year they were in a milk churn and another year in a little chest of drawers, and when you pulled out the drawers, the chocolates were in each of these.

(H.F.)

*Mr Iliffe and Jim, Harry's older brother, outside their house on Church Street.*

## A Child's Passport to Wonderland

While I was at the junior school, Victoria Street Junior, in the top class, the library used to send a box of books round once a week and the good readers in the class were allowed to take one home. I was one of the good readers. I must have been standing bewildered by this box of books and the teacher said, 'Try this one; it's a good story'. She sent me home with *The Wind in the Willows* and I have never been so disappointed. Really what I wanted was *Biggles* and things like that. At that time the school could recommend you for a library ticket, provided your parents agreed. So I took this card home requiring my mother and my father's signatures. Well, my father never had anything to do with anything that needed putting a signature on it, and me mother was very suspicious of any kind of form, largely because, I think, she didn't understand them. It took my brother, who was eight years older than me, to say, 'It's perfectly all right for you to sign for it. It's only a library ticket, so he can go to the library'. I was on tenterhooks whether she was going to let me have it. Finally she signed it and I went to the library and I can remember it as one of the most wonderful

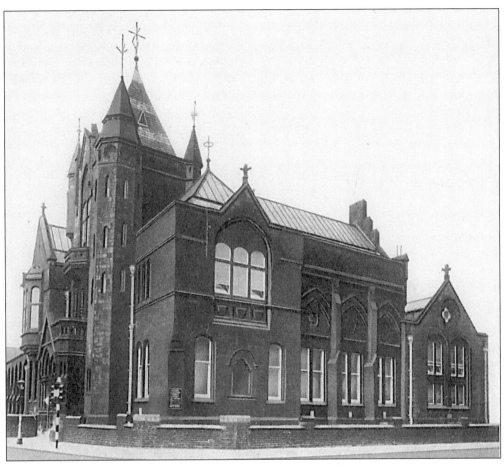

*Ashton Library.*

things in my childhood, actually getting a
library ticket and being able to go to the
library and get books out and come home
and read and read all these stories, because,
of course, you couldn't buy books at that
time. This was a really new experience and I
had a real affection for that library card. I
used to change my book – you were only
allowed one – every day. I went every night
and changed my book again and got another
one; of course, it was all the usual stuff, *Just
William* and *Biggles* and all that kind of
thing. But I thought it was magical. There
was a particular journey from [my house on]

Church Street to the library. If you went
onto Stamford Street there was a bike shop
with a narrow ginnel down the side of it; if
you went down that ginnel, it let you in the
back yards of the shops on Stamford Street.
You made your way hurriedly along there,
along their back yards, and then, if you
crossed behind Arcadia, there was an air
raid shelter, an underground air raid shelter
there. You went through this air raid shelter,
and up the escape ladder at the other end
and then across Old Street and into the
library. Opposite the library was an old book
shop – I think it was called Needham's – run

23

by a very old man. If there was more than one of you had gone to the library, you'd stick your head into Mr Needham's on the way back and get him to throw you out. He knew you didn't want to buy anything; you were just coming in to be a nuisance. Then you'd make your way back home, through the air raid shelter, down the back yards of the shops, up the ginnel and out again. If my mother knew the ways I went through these places, she'd never have let me have the library ticket in the first place.

(H.I.)

## Bursting the Gas Tar Bubbles

The roads were cobbled and the cobbles were all joined together in the middle of the road by gas tar. So you popped all these gas tar bubbles and then you went home. My mother used to give me a clout because it cost butter to get all this gas tar off wherever it had gone. It used to get on your clothes as well.

(E.B.)

## A Little Boy's Dream

In the Avenue there was a toyshop – Lumb's, was it? In the side window there was a model railway layout, sometimes with the trains going. I used to stand there with me nose pressed against that window, watching that railway, knowing full well I couldn't ask my parents for anything like that, 'cos I knew we couldn't afford it. That railway set really did fascinate me for years. If I was ever sent up Ashton, I always went via that window.

(H.I.)

## The Great Explosion

I must have been about six or seven. Oxford Street, Ann Street, Clyde Street, Portugal Street and Hamilton Street, and that row they call 'The Fine Ladies Row' all belonged to Mason's Mill, all the houses and everything. We had our own park that belonged to Mason's Mill. I was in the park one day, playing on the swings, and there was a terrific explosion. I dashed home and me mother was in an awful state; all the windows in the house were broken. Me father, who was an engine driver for Great Central Railway, was working at Guide Bridge sidings. He left his engine and he came running and he took us out of the house towards the other side of Trafalgar Square. All the windows broken, slates blown off the roof, everything was in a terrible mess.

(F.H.)

## Albert the Diplomat

I could get into trouble just by being good and telling the truth. There were three fish and chip shops within about a 100yds of our house on Hill Street. Mrs Barlow's was at the corner of Welbeck and Victoria Streets, Mrs Kershaw's at the corner of Welbeck and Park Streets and Arthur Giles' in Portland Street near Park Street. The counter in fish and chip shops used to be rather high, except for a small portion that was kids' size. I had stood quite some time waiting my turn at the kid's counter in Mrs Kershaw's and been overlooked. So I mentioned that I thought it was my turn, only to be told that the adults were coming home from work and I had plenty of time. I told her that I had

*The old fire station, Wellington Road.*

other errands to do also.

'Oh', said Mrs Kershaw, 'and where else have you to go, Albert?' I told her that I had to go to Mrs Barlow's for a fish for my granny's tea. 'I sell fish as well as chips, you know', she replied. 'Yes, I know', I said, 'my granny likes your chips but she likes Mrs Barlow's fish better'. The woman who relayed the story to Mam reckoned the shop full of people thought it was the funniest thing they had heard for a long time. Mrs Kershaw, though, didn't see the funny side of the episode.

Mrs Taylor's corner shop was opposite Mrs Barlow's fish shop. The shop window faced due west and it got the full afternoon sun. This made all the toffees in their jars very sticky. Mrs Barlow used to make these up into 'lucky bags' for the kids to choose for their halfpennies. My Mam considered these were poor value. When I went into Mrs Taylor's shop, she commented that she hadn't seen me in her shop for quite a while. 'My Mam said I wasn't to come in your shop anymore. You sell nothing, only muck'

(A.S.)

## You've Never Been Right Since

The first memory I have is just before I was three. On that day I remember a lady in a blue gown scurrying upstairs because that was the day my sister was born. I also remember having to walk behind the pram she was being pushed in and finding it very hard on my little legs. Our kitchen was a flag floor with coconut matting. I'm told I survived falling out of my high chair at the age of eighteen months and they say I've never been right since. After that my father would never let any child or grandchild be seen in any part of the high chair without being strapped in.

(J.M.)

## Child Star!

I played all the small parts. The teachers at West End, where I went to school, all went to the theatre. So, when they saw me on stage, the morning after it would be 'Come here, Margaret. We saw you last night. You were very, very good. They made a fuss of me and, once they knew that I could act, I had the lead in all the school plays. I got £3 for playing child parts in the theatre – 'Daddy Longlegs', and 'Alias Jimmy Valentine'. I can't remember the others. Stepmother always said, 'When they give you your money, put it in the hem of your coat in the dressing room'. That £3 then was an awful lot of money.

(M.B.)

## 'Don't Forget Your Passport'

When my grandma lived on Oxford Street, my father used to stand me on the gate opposite their house, which looked across the canal and the river and then up a hill to some houses at the top. He used to point to those houses and say, 'Those houses are in Dukinfield. Dukinfield is another town and it's in another county'. (Dukinfield was in Cheshire then). I thought he meant another country. So I always thought Dukinfield was a foreign country. Years later, when I was first doing my student teaching, I went to Globe Lane School in Dukinfield. When I used to leave home in the morning, they used to shout, 'Don't forget your passport'.

(H.F.)

## The Paper Boy

I delivered papers from being eleven years old for a lady on Whiteacre Road called Mrs Fowler. I did it to bring a bit o' money in the house. I used to start at half past six in the morning taking papers out and finish about quarter to eight. We also took papers at night. I was able to get a bike then out of my paper money. We used to go to Charlestown station to catch the train on which the *Evening News* and *Evening Chronicle* arrived.

(D.J.)

## Hitching a Ride

The one-man tram ran up Henrietta Street, along Canterbury Street, up Union Road to Hurst Cross, down Queen's Road, down Mossley Road, Penny Meadow, back into Ashton. There was only one man in charge. So, I, daredevil, used to wait at the bottom of Henrietta Street, catch on back when it set off, and ride up. I also used to catch lorries. Used to go to the corner of Mossley Road, Curzon Road; the big lorries were coming up, going about twenty miles an hour. I used to catch on the back of them. I've gone as far as Huddersfield.

(D.J.)

*Ashton tram on Union Road-Hurst route.*

## The Ghosts of Lees Road

One of the girls who was in the Rangers at Albion lived at the Red House, a public house on Lees Road. She'd come to the meeting and she'd forgotten something, so I would go with her [to get it]. We went on the tram or bus to Hurst Cross. Lees Road wasn't paved then. It was pitch black. As we were going along we could see something white bobbing about. 'What's that?', I said. Then we could hear voices. It was only a football team coming from the pub, running, having their exercises. It was a bit scary.

(Mrs A.B.)

# CHAPTER 2

## Schooldays

*The Jones family. The soldier is Percy Jones, who taught his nephew, David, to read.*

### Nellie Goes to School

I'd be about three; me mother and father were in cotton, and I were being minded from one neighbour to another (there were no nurseries and all that carry-on). We had a school on Union Road, just up there. In summertime they had their lessons in grounds, and it were all like country. Every day I used to go up and get in a little gate, where I shouldn't 'a done. So one day I got in and what did I do? I went and joined in line with little 'uns. This teacher – she were very tall – Miss Taylor, she knew me, with passing our door each day. She used to say, 'Hello, Nellie. Are you still lonely?' And I used to say, 'Yes, Miss'. So she says, 'Do you want to come to our school?' 'Ooh', I says, 'Yes please'. Well, she used to call for me every morning, coming up street. Me mother used to say, 'Have you played today, love?' I says, 'No! I've been to school'. And they took no notice of me.

(E.M.)

## Learning to Read

Education meant a lot. Uncle Percy, my dad's brother, he lived on Princess Street with my grandma. He used to have me up two or three nights a week, learning to read, things like *David Copperfield* or *Tom Sawyer* and all these books. I remember the gaslight, no sitting down, stand up at the table and read. He kept me busy there.

(D.J.)

## St James' School

I went to St James' School on Romney Street. Before that I started at the Albion School; something must have gone wrong and I said I wasn't going again. So my mother took me to St James'. The first teachers we had in the Infants were two Miss Revels, two sisters. The headmistress was Miss Wardle, and there was Miss Mee. Mr Humphries was headmaster in the Seniors and there was a Mr Day there; oh, and Mrs Pringle. I used to like her, because some days I used to go and stay at my grandma's on Warrington Street. Mrs Pringle came on the train to Park Bridge station and I used to walk to school with her. I used to think it was great, walking all that way to school with the teacher. She was a really nice lady.

(A.B.)

## Gatefield School

I went to Gatefield School. It's a garage now; it's still there. They were very, very strict. There was one teacher in particular –

when you did your maths, if you didn't do them right, you got a tap on the ear. I don't remember any of us ever having to go the headmaster for doing anything. If you went to the headmaster, you got four strokes. So we were all frightened to death; me mother were enough! He was called Mr Robson, the headmaster at Gatefield School.

(M.W.)

## St John's Junior and Heginbottom Modern

The junior school of St John's was in a large hall. You went there from five years old. There was only one teacher for all the different age groups in that junior school. When we moved into the other one, where Mrs Taylor was the Headmistress, there were four classes, I think. But it was a partition across the room. It wasn't a [separate] room. You only had one teacher, who took all the subjects. I remember writing on slates. When I became eleven years old, I sat the examination for the Grammar School, but me mother wouldn't let me go because neither of my sisters had been. I recollect the headmistress saying, 'Well, you're not going to Stamford. You'll go to Heginbottom Modern'. I thought, 'That's an awful long way to go down into Ashton'. Heginbottom Modern was part of the Ashton Library on Old Street there. There was also the Technical School there. There were two schools in one. My parents weren't wealthy. I had to walk. It must have been one and a quarter miles, and I walked home at lunchtime as well. I went down King's Road, Union Road, under the railway bridge, across the market – that was always an experience. I've dawdled many a time there. [If you went down Penny Meadow] there was a policeman on point duty at the bottom and woe betide the lad who crossed without being told.

(H.C.)

## Monday Morning Games

I went to the Modern School. That was behind where Woolworth's was on Stamford Street. I went there 'till I was fourteen. We had no playground there. For netball and things we went across to where the library is now; behind the library was a big yard and we used to have our games in there. Monday morning we were marched across there for games.

(D.S.)

## Good Morning, Sir!

I went to St James. Mr Wood was headmaster. Mr Wood used to walk to school along Curzon Road, because he lived on Montague Road. Y'had to say 'Good Morning, Sir!', if you saw Mr Wood – he were very strict. The other teachers I remember there – Mrs Cheetham, Miss Sutcliffe, Mrs Bradbury and Sam Batty (he were a popular one). I was one of the first scholars in Heginbottom Modern School, behind the library in Ashton. That's the school I went to till I was fourteen. That was quite a big change, the biggest change I ever had in my school days. At St James the teachers were ordinary people; but at Heginbottom Modern School every teacher wore cap and gown and always carried a stick. My first form master was a chap called Sutton, a young man and quite good.

(D.J.)

## Mrs Holderness' Collars and Mr Buckley's Dinners

I went to Gatefield School. The teachers were mostly women. There were Miss Wolstencroft. She were very nice; she lived in Mottram. Once a year they sold these pansies – blue pansies. I remember selling some of them for her, y'know, how they used to do Saturdays. Mrs Holderness used to send me to Blandford Street, with her husband's collars, to have 'em starched. I liked that, because I either got some very expensive chocolates or a drink of Horlicks. I preferred the Horlicks! Oh, and another thing. Mr Buckley, he came from Denton, and he used to bring his dinner in a dish, and he had me going home and warming it. I think I forgot to put the gas on once, so he never asked me again.

(A.A.)

## He's No Clogs, Sir!

Canon Johnson used to take the register Monday morning. If so and so was missing, 'Where is he?' 'He can't come, Sir. He's no clogs'. Then he'd call the girls. They'd no shoes t'come to school in. But they were there in the afternoon. He'd send them up to the cloggers, just up facing Billy Garside's there [the Dog and Partridge]: Albert Leech's clog shop, and they'd come to school in the afternoon and they had clogs on.

(N.B.)

## Buttercups and Daisies

I went to school at St Stephen's, that's just over the border in Audenshaw. I can remember the teachers. We had a Miss Swallow; she was the daughter of the vicar at that time. I remember having sticky paper that you used to fold, and then into little squares and cut things out from that. And then you learned your alphabet. We had little shells – y'know those shells that you hear the sea. I think we learned to count with these. I think we used pencils until we got a bit higher, in the top class of the babies, and then I think we used pens. We learned little rhymes like:

> Buttercups and daisies,
> oh what pretty flowers,
> Coming in the Springtime
> to tell us sunny hours.

(I.S.)

## Bookbinding and Singing Lessons

When we got into the upper classes we used to do a bit of bookbinding. The man who was the teacher then – Mr Stoddard he was called – had a singing lesson. We used to take old books apart and then set them out in volumes, and then put the canvas on the back. Then they was clamped down on a frame and we used to glue them and put the backs on.

[For the singing lessons] there wasn't a piano in the room. He used to give you a chord and you had to pitch up to it.

(E.C.)

## Double Punishment

I was only caned once. Me father, he was on nights that week. When I got home I complained to him that I'd been caned, and he said to me, 'If you don't behave yourself in school, I'll give you a good hiding'.

(F.H.)

## Look at Hilda!

My sister was very particular and always wore everything that matched, and I didn't care. My mother used to knit us these little suits. You had a skirt and a cardigan and a hat to match. You had a red one, a green one and a blue one. My mother wasn't very good at getting up in the morning. As soon as we were old enough, we'd get up and dress ourselves. I went to school one day and the headmistress (she was called Miss Booth) gave me a note to take round to the teachers. Being clever, I read it. It said on it, 'Just look at Hilda. Her mother hasn't seen her come out this morning'. I was wearing things that didn't match. I had one colour of skirt and another colour of top. I daren't admit to the teacher that I'd read the note. So I had to go round, and every teacher had to read this note and look at me and smile, then give it back. Then I had to go and give it to somebody else.

(H.F.)

## Beds and Umbrellas

I went to West End School. I never stayed dinners; me mother used to come for me and take me home. At first, when I went to school, we had beds. I went when I was three and a half and they had beds in the afternoon. Y'had to lie down and have a sleep every afternoon. Y'all had a picture –

mine was an umbrella. That was on your hook, your bed; everything at school had your picture on. I suppose, going at three and a half, you couldn't read. So from the picture, you knew everything that was yours.

(G.W.)

## Having a Nap in the Afternoon

I remember going to Trafalgar Square Infants' School with me brother – I must have been before infant school age, maybe about four – and I remember getting the beds out in the afternoon and having a sleep. I went to that school from five; then I went to West End Council School to being eleven. I was in Warrington House, which was blue.

(A.B.).

## I Shall Tell About You

We used to have cocoa. We had a fire-guarded fire in the infants' class. We used to have slates and scratchy pencils. I remember the cloakroom, and I remember the difficulty, at five, of dressing, because I used to wear some leather leggings with lots of buttons on. I can remember people appearing at school without shoes on, people having haircuts with a basin, people with very nearly shaven hair and people with very tatty clothing. Then there was the smell of the cloakroom, a mixture of dirty clothes and dust and whatever the caretaker cleaned it with. There were thick pipes around the room which we used to sit on to keep warm. There were three classes there. It was a school which had not long been built in the 1920s, with those tiled dadoes and upper walls – quite well built: Accrington brick. It had a very strict regime; if we ever did things that we were not expected to do, not only were there teachers there, but the caretaker was also a little … 'I shall tell about you'. So you didn't do it again; if you did, he told about you. If you took a short cut home across a field – which we were not supposed to do – the caretaker told tales. I got strapped on my backside for that, with a strap. The naughty boys got the cane in the infants.

(J.M.)

## The Unhappiest Days of My Life

I went to St James'; I'd just started when the war started. I went there till me moved to Cambridge Street; then I went to West End. St James' – I wasn't happy there at all. The main teacher was Mrs Artingstall. The man who became the headmaster was in me dad's class when me dad went to that school. Because the war was on and my father was away, my mother would never let me know anything about how the war was going on, or how the armies were doing. So I knew nothing about the war. Then you got these questions that you had to answer about the war. I never knew any answers, so I always had to stand on my chair. I wasn't the only one. I was always running home to me mum. Then you got the cane. I got the cane a lot because I was left-handed. When it was sewing class I had to stand outside [because] I can't sew the same way as everybody else. It was a very bad time for left-handed people.

(E.B.)

*West End School, 1946. The teachers are Miss Taylor, in the striped blazer, and Mrs Welles. Grace Wardle is on the back row, third from left.*

## West End Cowshed

First of all I went to St Peter's Infants' School on Welbeck Street; then to St Peter's Junior on Victoria Street, where I did the 11+ and failed; then from there to West End Council School. We referred to it as 'The West End Cowshed'. It was wartime, so all the teachers at that time were people who effectively had been brought back out of retirement, because all the younger teachers had been taken away into the forces. Quite a lot of the things that the school normally did couldn't be done because of the war. There was no wood until the last few months before I finished school, so they couldn't have Woodwork lessons. So, in the top class, we used to be sent across on a Friday afternoon to the girls' side, and do cookery instead of woodwork. You had to ask your mum for some of the rations to do cookery, which you spoiled and brought home burned and whatever. The headmaster some time before I

left was called Jones. I was a prefect in my last year and I helped to teach a lot of evacuees how to read. There were quite a number in the school from London, and most of them, although they were very nearly ready to leave school, couldn't read 'CAT' etc. So I was doing basic things with them. The headmaster used to say, 'If I can get these lads out of here able to read and add up their wages at the weekend, I think I'll have done a good job'.

(H.I.)

## The Illegal Player

I'd left Christchurch School eighteen months to two years and I were butchering on Oldham Road. I were always a good footballer. Th' headmaster from Christchurch come in and he says, 'Buck, d'you think you could do me a favour? We

*West End Senior School (Girls) Class 1A, c. 1938.*

got a good beating by a Glossop team last week, and we're going for a return match up their place this coming Friday. Would you play for us?' I says, 'I've left school eighteen months'. He says, 'They'll not be able to tell'. So anyway we goes up and plays this team. We lost and after the match a chap come across and he said, 'Didn't see you when we played at Waterloo'. 'No', I said, 'I were off poorly'.

(N.B.)

## Half a League

We went up to Stamford School there and Mr Duncan was the headmaster. All I remember about Mr Duncan is he used to come in our class one morning a week and recite the poem *The Charge of the Light Brigade*. All I remember is him saying, 'Half a league, half a league, into the valley of death', and then he went.

(B.P)

## Elgin Street School and the Film Man

I went to school very early. My brother going, I must have missed him, so I just walked my way in once. I started about a year early. That was at Elgin Street, at the back of Minto Street. It's still going; Canon Johnson I think they call it now. There was a chap who lived at the back. He used to put these film shows on in the back yard, and he used to charge children. I would probably be the youngest there.

(D.F.)

## Scholarship Girl

I went to St James' Day School and, when I was eleven, I had to sit the exam. They took us to sit this exam – y'know the library on Old Street? Well, next to it was a school and we had to go in there to sit this exam. I passed. I'd won a scholarship, given by a tripe merchant on George Street. He had a tripe shop and he'd given this scholarship. He provided all the money for me books etc., which was a good thing because me dad came out of work later on. So I started at the Grammar School. I did all right. I was going to go in for teaching. My father worked at the National. He'd been on three days for ages; then he got stopped altogether. I was sixteen; I was going to go on to [teacher] training college. But he came out of work, and there was no income coming in; me auntie had finished work and there was me granddad. So I had to leave school and get a job. So where did I go? Robertson's Jam Works, in the warehouse! That was the only job I could get at the time.

(Mrs E.C.)

## Getting the Soup Home

At the Grammar School we actually did war service, 'cos we used to go across to the Infirmary and make cocoa in the evenings. I remember the ward where we were on duty. I took Domestic Science as one of my subjects. We used to make things like potato soup and carrot soup. If you rode a bicycle, and you had your school bag – and we wore those big velour hats that blew off in the wind – and you were also trying to juggle potato soup to take home, it wasn't very good. There was a little grid at the end of Queen's Road, and we used to pour our soup down there when we were setting off.

(H.F.)

Hurst Methodist School, 1935. The fair-haired boy at the extreme left of the third row back is Bob Parkinson.

*Stamford Boys' School sports team, c. 1946.*

## The Grammar School in Wartime

The year started by a sort of open night, where we all had to go and buy second-hand text books that were handed down from the previous year, as people moved up. There was no new material at all, with the restrictions from the war. There were very few young teachers either; they were nearly all retired teachers. The headmaster was G.B Jackson, a very strict disciplinarian; but he did talk to us and we did feel that we were human and part of the same organization.

(A.B.)

## My Days at Hurst Brook School

I went to Hurst Brook-St James' School, which was on Union Road. We used t'have singing, music lessons and all that. I remember when we were in the infants'

school we had a slate, with a wooden thing around it; and you had a piece of chalk. Didn't have books in the infants' school. Miss Ainsworth was the headteacher and Jimmy Wood was the headmaster. He was also a JP and sat on the bench at Ashton. He used to say to us, 'Any of you come on my bench and I'll show you'. He didn't half put the fear of God in you. Most of the kids wore clogs. I especially remember wintertime. We got winters then. The schoolyard sloped down and we used to have long slides, right down to the bottom.

(B.N.)

## Ashton Technical College

I was quite surprised when I went to the Tech, because you had individual teachers, not one teacher who taught you everything. The headmaster, (they didn't call him the headmaster; they called him the principal) he didn't teach. It was like when you were in the army. If you did anything wrong, they'd send you to his office and you'd wait outside, and he'd hear the teacher's side of the story and then your side. The teacher's side was always accepted, of course, and you'd get a caning if you'd done anything wrong. The teachers wore their black gowns; even one or two of them wore mortar boards.

(J.E.)

*Ashton Grammar School.*

# CHAPTER 3

## Family Life

*David Jones' dad, aged about twenty.*

### A Father Lost Too Soon

My dad was a blacksmith by trade; he worked at a firm in Stalybridge, Scott and Hodsons. He had a fit – he suffered from epilepsy – and fell on a forge at work. He wasn't injured, but they couldn't chance him doing a job like that. So he was thrown out of work. So me mother she went to work, weaving at Crookbottom Mill. They used to start early in the morning in them days. Me dad was at home, and he bought a hen pen and kept hens, right next to Ormond Street church. When me mother went to work, he'd leave us in bed and go and feed his hens. Then he'd come back and get us up for school. One morning I woke up in bed and said to me sister, 'Me dad's late. We'd better get up'. So we got up and dad still hadn't

*David Jones (second from left) with his brothers, Arthur and Kenneth, and sister Alice in 1925.*

come. So our Alice and me walked down to the pen. We could get in the pen, but we couldn't get in the hen-cote, because there was a lock on the inside. So we didn't know what to do. We were coming out and there's some houses there and a woman called Mrs Hyde she saw us coming out and she said, 'What's matter?' We said, 'We can't get in the hen-cote. We can't make our dad hear us'. So they got the police down and they found me dad dead. He'd had a fit and he'd fell on his face and he'd suffocated. They had to send for me mother. There was no such thing as getting you back quick like. She had to catch the bus to come back home. I can see it now. She came up to where we lived – we lived in Bombay Street then – and she said, 'What is it? Joe?' That's how me dad died. Me mother coped mainly by taking in washing and ironing for people.

(D.J.)

## A Good-Living Man

My mum and dad didn't go to church. But me dad read his Bible every day. He was a good-living man. He was brought up a Catholic. I think that he went to the churches he played football for after that. He never missed reading his Bible. He didn't think he was good enough to go (to church). He was in hospital for quite a period. He knew all the ministers; he had a word with them all. He always said, 'If you can't say anything good about anybody, don't say anything'.

(D.S.)

## A Man of Some Importance

My father worked at the Co-op in Manchester. When the war came on he was in the coal department. Obviously there was a shortage (and) rationing. He was very lucky – he got this job at the Ministry, allocation of coal to all the coalmen around the North-West. He allocated how much they got and they had to keep in with him. I remember him getting big packets of cigarettes, and a turkey or something like that at Christmas. He got a car and everything. He was always out; I mean he was always being taken everywhere by these respective coal firms, just to keep in with him, y'see, to get an allocation. Once the war finished, he went back to his department in Balloon Street in Manchester. It was a big shock to him, a comedown from the money he was getting (as a coal allocator).

(D.F.)

## Father and the Three Minutes

When I were going out with me friends – even when I were courting – I had to be in at dead on ten o'clock. I were being married in a few months. I remember one night we went to Dendle's, where there were plays; oooh, they were good. I happened to look at the clock – five to ten. So I touched George and I said, 'Are you watching this play out?'. He says, 'Of course I'm watching' I says, 'Let me pass. I daren't stay '. And do you know, I set off running from theatre till I got up here. I were twenty-five then, twenty-five. Me father were reading, and he never lifted his eyes off paper. When I came in, d'you know what he says? 'What's happened to those three minutes?' I'm not lying. Me heart started beating. I can feel it yet.

(E.M.)

## We Must Be Home By Tea-time

Mother spent a lot of time taking us out, and she was a great one for collecting all the other children in the neighbourhood and taking those with her. We used to walk along Lees Road to what we called 'The Clough', or over the 'Coalpit Hills', which were at the back of the shops on Broadoak Road. We used to play in the Clough. A little stream ran through the bottom there. We used to collect tadpoles, nature things and things like that. My father worked at a mill in Droylsden and went on a bicycle. At exactly five minutes to six every night he came in through the garden gate, put his bicycle by the side of the wall and came round and his tea was ready for him. Whatever we did when we were children, we always had to be home in time for tea to be ready for five minutes to six.

(H.F.)

## Accident

Dad was an engineer at Daniel Adamson's. He was a turbine engineer and supervisor at the depot. One Friday afternoon a chain broke, or slipped, and a casting dropped across his body and rested on his legs. They saved his legs, but he had a lot of operations and he was in hospital for well over a year. He did go back to work, but he was never the same after that. Me mother went back to doing what she'd done in the early days of the family, taking in washing and things like that.

(A.B.)

## My Father the Musician

My dad was a wages clerk at Guide Bridge. He used to come home at 5.30, have his tea and have a nap. Then he'd get dressed - evening dress - and then he'd go and play until 11.30 and 12.30 at night. Sunday morning he had a band at the Trades Club. His orchestra used to go around all the churches for their school anniversaries and play for all of them. I can see him now, with all his orchestra, at Trafalgar Square Church. It used to be beautiful.

(M.B.)

## Father and the Roller Towel

Monday morning were Black Monday in our house, when he'd had a few cutties on Sunday night. Who did he take it out on? Nellie! One Monday morning, when I were drying me hands and face, father said, 'Nellie, this roller towel needs changing' (Y'know, they had 'em behind door then, on rollers".) 'In a minute', I said. He came towards me. Me brother, our Billy, he thought he were going t'hit me. So me brother, he gets hold of his braces and pulls him back, them being elastic. He always said our Billy hit him.

(E.M.)

## Buying Furniture

At that time me mother used to get her furniture by having a firm call round. It was a family firm. They used to call on Friday night and I think she used to pay them six pence. Lots of people used to do this. When they'd finished paying for one piece of furniture, they thought what they'd like to renew next. They just carried on and they got the next piece of furniture and paid, and when they were getting to the end of paying sixpences for that, the man coming round would say, 'You've only got another three weeks, Mrs Iliffe', and my mother would sort of say, 'Do with a new piece of carpet next'. He didn't charge interest on the loan. They just paid weekly for them at the shop price. The firm made its money by having regular customers. I can remember getting a three piece suite like that. Nobody thought it was unusual; it was just normal.

(H.I.)

## Mother, Brother and the Muffins

Mother did her own baking for a number of years. She used to work and do her own

William 'Billy' Wood.

*William 'Billy' Wood aged about twenty-one.*

washing and bake three times a week – big bowls in the front of the fire, and all the tins rising and then muffins. Me brother used to come in and he used to take the muffins out hot, with jam on. I used to say, 'Is he eating all of them?', and she says, 'No, he's giving them to his mates'. Once he said that everywhere were mucked up (with the baking). So she never baked again.

(A.A.)

## My Mum, the Gardener

I can always remember going to Stamford Park on Sunday mornings, with me dad pushing the pram. Me dad would have his walking stick and a bowler hat on. My mother had an allotment on Beaufort Road,

where the college is now and we used to spend hours down there. It was really nice. She loved her garden, me mum. She built a little shed to put her things in.

(Mrs A.B.)

## Breaking Her Pledge

My mother worked in the mill, but she gave up work when my eldest sister was born. She didn't go to work again until during the war, when she took over an insurance book for somebody who was going into the forces. She worked on that something like two evenings and a Saturday morning. Sometimes we used to go with her; she didn't take my elder sister and I at the same time; she only took one of us. It was a great treat to go round with mum and do the collecting, 'cos she collected round the streets of Ashton itself, behind the old *Reporter* office and the George and Dragon. She was very teetotal, a member of the Temperance and the Band of Hope. She went in about six pubs (collecting insurance) and was once seen coming out of one. She was accused of breaking her pledge.

(H.F.)

## Our Mother, the Actress

Mother was on the stage and was well-known. Evelyn Kington – that was her stage name. She was a child star. She'd acted with some of the big names; she'd acted with Rob Wilton.

(M.B. and A.G.)

## See if She'll Give Us a Sub

When me sister and I had started work, for every shilling we earned, we'd have a penny spending money; at least, that was the basis mother went on. Of course, like all youngsters, by Thursday we were broke. The Roxy cinema had opened by then. My sisters used to say – I was the favourite, being the boy – 'Slink in, will you, and see if she'll give us a sub'. That was so that we could go to the Roxy on a Thursday night. And she would. And when it came to [next week's] spending money, she never deducted it.

(H.C.)

## Fine Ladies' Row and the Drying Ground

The building they call the Twelve Apostles now, used to be called Fine Ladies' Row. A lot of the men who worked at the Oxford Mill, who had overlookers' and better jobs, lived in that row. Their wives were the fine ladies', hence Fine Ladies' Row. At the back of Fine Ladies' row there was a big, wide, open space. It was known as the Drying Ground, 'cos the ladies used to put their washing in there. There were stumps they could put their lines on. They called it the Drying Ground.

(F.H.)

## Rough Times

This big explosion was down what they call Ryecroft. I remember I was about nine years old. I was playing on the outside front when the bang went off. I ran in the house. My father was at the 1914-18 war. Of course, me

mother was there and me grandma. Me mother had a confinement and the doctor had only brought one baby and left the other one in, and it mortified. She'd had to be rushed to St Mary's Hospital. She'd come back [when the explosion happened] and was in bed. It [the explosion] blew her out of bed and onto the floor. We five children then was all under me grandmother's care. Me dad came home from the forces; he got special leave to come home to me mother. He overstayed his leave and the military came to collect him. He had to go back. He did tell us that when he went back he was strapped to the wheel for twenty-four hours. That was the punishment. Anyhow, me

The actress Evelyn Kington, stepmother to Alice and Margaret Wood.

43

mother did live; but the children, the babies, they died.

(M.W.)

## Old Stockings and Glass Feet

We used to put old stockings on the table legs, and they (the stockings) came off on Sundays. They were put on every Sunday night so the legs wouldn't get scratched during the week. And the best fender came out on Sundays. They used to put glass feet under the piano legs, to preserve the carpet. But the glass feet made more impression than the castors on the piano.

(M.B.)

## Clothing My Boys

Me mother was very keen against credit. The only credit she used – Arcadia used to run a club, and you paid so much into the club every week. Before you paid the full amount, you could spend that money. For example, if it was a twelve-week club, after six or seven weeks you could spend that money. That's how mother used to clothe us. At Whitsuntide she always used to go to Lewis' in Manchester, to buy us raincoats and whatnot.

(H.K.)

## Baking Bread and Getting the Bird for Christmas

Mother used to bake her own bread. She had in the living room a bungalow range,

beautifully black-leaded. I suppose it was quite old really. I remember the big earthenware pot at the side of the fire, waiting for the yeast to make it rise. I remember having to clean bungalow range as well – spit and polish! When we were younger and there were war restrictions, mother used to go to Manchester queuing up at the fowl market to see what sort of bird she could get us for Christmas. She would go several times before she struck lucky.

(A.B.)

## Knowing Her Place

My mother and father used to go up the Old Nook pub; that was the only recreation they had. Me mother always walked three paces behind me dad. [He had his] hard hat on, well and truly brushed before they went out. Shoes were always clean. She was an organizer, me mother. She'd organize trips from the pub, to go on outings, that kind of thing. She used to say to me dad, 'Take a chance; take a chance'. He never would.

(H.C.)

## Me Mum!

If me mother said, 'I'll see', you usually thought she was going to say 'Yes'. Me dad always used to say, 'Ask your mother', if we asked him if we could go anywhere. I've had a real lot of good smackings, but I always deserved it. Me mother was very, very hard working. She had two men to wash and iron for and us to look after; she washed for other people; and she cleaned at a pub as well. She always tried to do things where she didn't have to leave us, because her mother had always had to go out to work and leave her, because she had no father. She didn't want to leave us, so she worked for a lot less than she needed to, so that she didn't have to leave us. She'd go and take papers for the paper shop before we went to school in a morning. Then she cleaned at this pub in the mornings. I've never known anybody do as much cooking and baking as she did; everything was homemade. She cleaned, and when she cleaned everything was cleaned well.

(G.W.)

## Grandfather

My grandfather Millin was the local carter for the Lancashire and Yorkshire Railway. He had a horse in Charlestown, in the stables there, where there's these big warehouses. He worked out of Oldham Road Goods Yard. He delivered to Kerfoots, the Rock Mill, Atlas Mill … he used to save all the packing cases and everything. He used to smoke a pipe; he never drank; and he saved all his money. He bought his first house. He had a little pen and a big garden, where my grandmother used to have raspberry canes and strawberries and flowers. He had a hen pen, and eggs. When I had a bike [it was my job to] take all the eggs out to the customers on a Saturday morning. He had another hen-pen, and he used to fence it with all these skip sides and bits and pieces. He used to keep the local butcher's lambs there on the hoof, before he killed them. I always remember, he'd be in his little workshop in his hen-pen, and he'd be de-nailing all these things, straightening nails, putting them into different sizes, wrapping up string. He saved everything: 'It'll come in someday'.

(J.M.)

*Mrs Janet Wardle, mother of Grace and Joyce (later Iliffe).*

## Great-Grandmother

On Littlemoss was my great-grandmother Greenwood. She was originally a Warren. She was the last unqualified midwife in our area. I had her little black bag once. She brought people into the world and she laid them out as well. As far as folk-medicine was concerned, handed down from generation to generation, she knew everything. She was an old lady with long black skirts. My uncle used to pick me up after Sunday school and take me round there on Sunday mornings. That was an old house! Flycatchers, upright wringing machines, flag floor, and a maiden aunt who lived with her, who was very deaf. That was fascinating – always a biscuit, always lemonade, home-made lemonade, and always scrupulously clean. The house is still there at Littlemoss, opposite Back Lane.

(J.M.)

## A Careful Grandma

I used to be taken into Ashton. I could be taken by either grandmother. My grandmother Millin would get off [the bus] at Atlas Street. I used to say, 'Why are we getting off here?' 'Because it's another halfpenny if you go to Oldham Road. It's only a penny here'. We used to walk the rest of it. My other grandmother must have been a bit better off, because we used to get off at Newmarket Road and had a shorter walk.

(J.M.)

## Getting Grandpa to Bed

When we went to live with my grandpa, he wouldn't go to bed at night. We three girls wanted him to go, so we could have a bit of peace. We had gas-mantles. We used to tie a bit of cotton around the thing and keep pulling it so that the mantle would go out. Or we'd take the penny. Once the penny went, he went to bed. He always sat right round the fire, so we wouldn't see it.

(A.G.)

## Never Mind, Grandfather

I were jealous of anybody going near me grandfather. I loved him. He said to me once, 'Do you know, dear, if I had my life over again, I'd have no children, none to make you laugh, none to make you cry'. I remember, when he died, me grandmother coming knocking on bedroom door. She said, 'Joseph, your father's in lavatory and I can't get him out'. So me father rushed downstairs and he couldn't loosen the door. So he took door off and me grandfather dropped dead between me father's legs. Me father never worked for twelve months after that – nervous debility. They fetched [me grandfather] in and laid him on the couch and I didn't know he were dead. I were getting water and I were bathing his head (where he fell, he was bleeding from his head). I were saying, 'Never mind, grandfather. You'll be better when you waken up'. It were only six o'clock in the morning. I were in me nightdress, bathing him, and a policeman come in and he come to me, and I always remember him saying, 'You poor little child'. When I got to know that he were dead, I never went to bed until they buried him. I were sitting on stairs; I couldn't go to bed. [At his funeral] there were so many grandchildren and great grandchildren. I couldn't understand it. My father were next to youngest child and I were next to the back. I couldn't understand it – living with him and being on back row. I felt I should have been up front with grandfather. I loved him so much.

(E.M.)

## The Sister I Never Knew

I had a sister that I never knew. She was born between me and my brother. She

*Harry Iliffe and his mum in the doorway of their house on Church Street.*

died of meningitis. She got meningitis and was taken to hospital in Manchester; I think it were Garside Street Children's Hospital. When my mother got there, out of the ambulance, she was told that my sister was dead already. She actually brought her home on the tram, although she'd died. She brought her home on the tram; she'd only had an ambulance going there. She came back with her in her arms. Then, when it came to arranging for a funeral, of course, me mother and father – I don't think my father was working at that time – had my sister buried in a neighbour's grave in the church at Guide Bridge, in St Stephen's churchyard. She was in someone else's grave, who kindly let her be buried in the grave because my mother and father couldn't afford one.

(H.I.)

## My Sister's Clogs

I remember my mum buying me some clogs. I was five, I remember, and I was thrilled to bits, y'know, at the noise they made in the street. I thought it was lovely, and my sister was most ashamed. She hated them. She hated going to school because she'd got these clogs. I don't think she wore them long, but she was ashamed of having to wear clogs. I suppose my mum thought they'd last longer than shoes. We must have been pretty poor, but I didn't realize it. I mean, everybody else was the same. I think I got a Friday penny and a Saturday tuppence, and that was my lot. But I was quite happy. Nobody else had any money, so it didn't bother you.

(D.S.)

## Our New Toboggan

My mother went out shopping one day when it was snowing. When she came back we were tobogganing down Broadbent Avenue. 'Where've you got your toboggan from?' 'Dad made it'. Mum and dad had done some ice-skating at one time, and they each had a pair of ice-skates; they were in a cupboard at home. In the kitchen we had a table that had a middle bit and two leaves. Because of space and all the other things you had to fit in, one leaf was always down, and it was pushed up against a sideboard. The other leaf lifted up when we were eating. When mum went in the house, dad had taken the leaf off the table and sawed it in half, and put it together and put four ice-skates on the bottom of it to make the toboggan. There was a big row, because he'd ruined the table. 'You never used it anyway'. But mum was saying, 'That's not the point. It was a piece of furniture'.

(H.F.)

*Oakfold Avenue at the junction with Broadbent Avenue.*

## The Family's Sunday Outing

We lived on Margaret Street, and, on Sundays, the family outing was to walk up Stamford Street, turn at the top – is it Bow Street or George Street? – and walk back down Old Street. That was the family outing, after we'd come from Sunday school. Lots of people did the same walk that we did, and looked in all the shop windows.

(J.I.)

## Going on Holiday

We went to Blackpool at Ashton Wakes. You didn't go boarding. You took your own stuff with you. The landlady cooked your meals for you, but you gave her what you wanted. You paid so much for your bed. You provided your own food and you had a little shelf in the dining room where you put your salt and pepper and sugar and things like that. You'd take perhaps a half dozen eggs and give her the bacon and she'd do the breakfast for you. The bread – I used to call it Blackpool bread – they were big, round rolls and I loved it. It was nice and, of course, you bought it fresh.

(D.S.)

## Just a Way of Life

In late 1945 we moved to a house just off Whiteacre Road, where the pub, the Half Way House, is still there. The street was called Holden Street and it ran right down (it was downhill all the way) as far as King George's Playing Fields and Hurst Laundry. The street's long gone. The only stretch of it left is where Hurst laundry is now. Right at the side of Holden Street they had what we used to call 'The Croft', a piece of open ground; and there was a tripe works there, Arnold and Hough's UCP Tripe. That area around Whiteacre Road was very nice. They were all poor people. That is why we often joke about the fact that in those days nobody used to lock their doors. You'd be sat in the house and suddenly you'd hear the front door open and a voice would say, 'It's only me'. It would be one of the neighbours. Everybody did this. Nobody locked their doors. You never heard of any burglaries. When you think about it, the reason why there was no crime or violence was that nobody had anything worth stealing. The most valuable piece of property was probably a radio. Nobody had any money. You didn't have to worry about money 'cos you hadn't got any. Just a way of life. It was old property, but the people were great.

(J.E.)

## Flitting

We lived at 26 Winter Street. I were born there, so were our Billy. Next door came empty. Me father says to me mother, 'I think we'll go and live next door. I'll get children up in morning and we'll flit. So we flitted in. We hadn't asked landlord. 'Oh', says me dad, 'Tommy'll be awreet on Saturday. I'll tell him'. So when Tommy came to Number 26 we weren't there. It were empty. We were in 28. We hadn't been in a great while and summat happened. Number 26 come empty again. So Dad says, 'We're going home. I don't like this so and so house. I don't think we're having any luck'. So we flitted back in the night.

(E.M.)

*Mrs Ethel Parkinson (third from left) with some friends outside Ashton Knitting Co. on Whitelands Road, 1944.*

## Means Test

My father died in 1932, so I don't remember him at all. Me mother worked at Hurst Mills before the war. Then she worked at Ashton Knitting Co., which was on Whitelands Road, until she retired. If you couldn't work and you had to look after a child, you had to go somewhere to get some money. I can remember going down to a place called the PSA, just off Penny Meadow. It was like a means test. Me mother got five shillings for herself and I got two and six pence. That was to live on for a week. That was just before the war. Then, of course, she went to work and she worked hard for whatever she had.

(B.P.)

## The House Before the Subway

I had a brother about four years older than me, and, when I was two and he was six, my father took us to live with his sister. You know Charlestown Station? There's a tunnel there, and I lived at the last house before you went under that tunnel. That's where this auntie lived – Auntie Ethel. She lived with her father. She worked in the mill. So, during the day, me grandfather had to look after us. We used to fall out, me and me brother. Granddad used to chase us. The house was at the bottom of Turner Lane. That subway tunnel breaks my heart as I go down it now. It's always dirty. I used to sweep that subway nearly every day.

(E.C.)

## Stoning the Street

I was born in 1913 and we lived in Marlborough Street. The house is no longer there. Marlborough Street ran from William

Street right up to Guide Bridge. Every house in Marlborough Street had stoned window sills, door-steps and flags. We used to wet them and mop them and then we stoned them with sandstone, till they were gleaming. On a Friday you could look the length of Marlborough Street and see the window sills and door-steps shining at every house.

(I.H.)

## Bribing Our Billy

Our Billy used to say, 'I've seen our Nellie talking to such-a-body'. I used to bribe him, and give him summat so he wouldn't tell me father. It's true. He'd take two bob off me for wiping pots, our Billy, so I could get out a bit sooner.

(E.M.)

## Life in the Crowthorne Hotel

Me dad finished on the railway and they decided to take the Crowthorne Hotel up, on Crowthorne Road, off Manchester Road. Me pals used to come round. They thought it was great that me mum had a pub. We used to live upstairs. The pub was all downstairs. Of course, after we finished drinking, we all used to go upstairs, take a few bottles with us and have a private party. Me mum and dad were only in there actually about four years. It got a bit too much for me mother. They bought a house in Hallam Street, just round the side, off Ryecroft Street.

(J.E.)

## The Strangler's Arms

There was a pub next door to Woolworths on Stamford Street. It got pulled down many years ago. It was the 'Prince of Wales' but we used to call it 'The Strangler's Arms' because there was a woman murdered there, just after the war.

(J.E.)

## The Black Knight Pageant

It was a regular thing for Ashton, on a special day. My dad was in it; he wore a pillbox hat and had a ginger 'tache. Him and Walter Cornes used to ride at front, at either side, before Black Knight came through on his horse. He had all coloured clothes on him. And then these girls were three this side, three that, side-saddle. All the tradesmen used to dress their lorries up then, well, the horses. The younger children would be at the end [of the procession] and they'd have these tassels waving. It was nearly a mile long, the pageant. It used to begin at the market place, go off the market, up towards Stamford Street, all round Stamford Street, back down Old Street, down onto Oldham Road, onto Wellington Road and then back to the market. It must have been three hours of a job, if you were waiting for it coming. There was very nearly everybody on the market when it set off – then they used to run to Old Street and see it again. It was spectacular.

(M.W.)

## The Legend of the Black Knight

The story about the Black Knight was that circa 1400, around Ashton, he was keen on

*Evelyn Kington taking part in the Black Knight Pageant.*

*Boys' Brigade in the Black Knight Pageant, c. 1948.*

the growth of wheat. He used to go round and, if he saw any wheat in fields, he used to summon the tenant, and he used to put them in a spiked barrel and roll them down the hill. The Black Knight Pageant was a parade, and there was a man who used to dress in armour. Between the two wars we used to live on Old Street. Part of the library was used as an Art School and every time there was a Black Knight Pageant, the students used to make medieval costumes. The Black Knight used to be a man called Clayton – he used to deliver ice to fish merchants and ice cream people. The Black Knight had a big black funeral horse. The pageant used to consist of his retinue, the Black Knight's court. There were jazz bands, twenty or thirty of those; there were horse drays dressed up. There were individual prizes. The pageant was in aid of the Infirmary.

(H.K.)

# Church

## The Tin Mission

Down near the warehouse at Portland Basin there was a place that we called the 'Tin Mission'. It was a corrugated iron building, quite a large building, and I used to go there

*One of the exhibits in the Black Knight Pageant in the 1930s.*

*Ashton Cooperative Society exhibit in the Black Knight Pageant in the 1930s.*

with friends. I've no idea what sect it belonged to. In the early war years certainly I oscillated between Henry Square Methodist and the Tin Mission. It was quite a large place and the little confectioner's round our corner, where we used to buy bread, they used to be part of the establishment of the Mission. The building is still there, but derelict.

(H.I.)

## Taunton Sunday School

I must have been taken to Taunton Sunday School very young. I was never on the cradle roll; my sister was the first one on the cradle roll. When they had a cradle at Whitsuntide processions they had this doll in it. Over the top of it was this cradle roll with everybody's name on it. Taunton Sunday School had a sloping floor, quite unique in itself, but bad for badminton, which they eventually played there. I also remember the knots in the floorboards, because, if you danced there – and there was always dances and whist drives – you had to dance round the knots. There was the main schoolroom, which had a dado and the pipes round it, and a radiator which said 'J.G.Wagstaff' on. There was a gallery, but children weren't allowed in the gallery unless they had adults with them. You had a star card that they used to stamp; then, when you got older, you had the job of stamping the star cards. I remember singing and the vapour of your voices came up because it was so cold and you never took your coats off. After the main service in the afternoon, the children's part, the young ladies came in and sat in, and the old ladies in their bonnets and black capes came in and sat there, and the men came back for the final hymns and prayers. On the children's pantomimes I was the stage manager. I remember, on one of those rehearsals, the death of King George V – that would be 1935 wouldn't it? . Then all the excitement of the Coronation, and little medals, and all the things which we got at that time. Also Robert Raikes' medals for Sunday School.

(J.M.)

## Albion Church

My great grandfather went to Albion church; he met my great grandmother there. I went to Albion church from being two or three weeks old. We went to Sunday school from being very young. If we didn't go with my mother, we went with my grandmother, who lived to be 105. The Sunday school was the one at the top of Penny Meadow. There was always something going on within the church; there was the Village Fair, which they used to have every year, and there was the pantomime at Christmas. I was in several but I was never known to be a very elegant dancer. Every year there was a Temperance exam, where you had to swot up on the evils of drink. The first school bag I had when I went to grammar school I bought with prize money from the Temperance exam.

(H.F.)

## The Village Fair

The Village Fair was held in the upstairs part of Albion and was a fundraiser for the church. Everybody had stalls, rather like they do now at the Christmas Fairs. They used to have different stalls, like the craft stalls. My mother always had the tripe stall. I suppose she got tripe in great big lumps and cut pieces off and weighed them up. We used to have home-bake stalls and things like that. My grandma told me of the time when they had a carousel, with horses on it and the children could ride round.

(H.F.)

## Sunday School at Trafalgar Church

Sunday school was wonderful. Sunday morning we went into Sunday school and then we went into church. And then Sunday school was Sunday school. People used to sit and talk to you in different groups. Mr Marshall was on the piano. You got a card to get a prize; you got stars stamped on it. Sunday night we all sat upstairs in church, all the boys on this side and all the girls on that, weighing the boys up. Then the choir was there, where the organ was. They used to have a marvellous choir. In those days we had a beautiful harvest set-up – all the vegetables and all the fruit. They used to hang the grapes where the organ was, and the red curtain round. The organist – he was a wonderful organist – used to sit eating the grapes. His name was Ephraim Hewitt. I always remember, after *The Messiah* they told you the collection. Once I remember them saying that over £90 had been taken. That was a lot of money.

(M.B. and A.G.)

*Trafalgar Square Methodist Church which was demolished in the 1960s.*

*A drawing of Henry Square Methodist Church, demolished in the 1960s.*

*Trafalgar Square Methodist Church Young People's Comradeship, 1935. The minister is Revd Ernest Hardy. Frank Harrison is fourth from right on second row from front.*

The Coming of Simon Evil. *Frank Harrison (far right) is Simon Evil.*

## I've Come to Sunday School

I started to play with Anita Shaw's brothers, and they used to go to Henry Square Church, so I started to go there. The first time I went in there on me own on a Sunday afternoon to Sunday school, there were no lights on. It was a very dark Sunday school; it always needed lights on. I went inside and there was this very tall man looking down at me. He said, 'What have you come for, lad?' 'I've come to Sunday school', I said. 'Well, it's not open yet. You've come too early'. I went back out again, and I didn't go back for a few weeks because he frightened me. His name was Joe Garlick, and I found out later that he was the Superintendent of the Sunday school. He was the kindliest man you could have known, a lovely man.

(H.I.)

## The Coming of Simon Evil

I went to Trafalgar Square church from being a child. I got to be one of the teachers and eventually the Superintendent of the Sunday school. We used to put plays on at church every year; one of them was called *The Coming of Simon Evil*, and I played Simon Evil.

(F.H.)

## Sunday School Outings

The adults at church treated us with parties etc and we went out once a year on a trip on a bus to Manor Park in Glossop. They hired a bus off SHMD and we went to Manor Park. There was always games, a few races and whatnot and prizes, which I never enjoyed. Sometimes there'd be a cricket

*Joe Garlick, 'the kindliest man you could have known', with his wife and children.*

*Trafalgar Square Methodist Church outing on a lorry with wooden wheels.*

match or people would just play around on the swings and paddle in the river. Directly opposite the gates of Manor Park was this Sunday school. We used to book that and you'd take your sandwiches in there and they'd brew tea. Then, afterwards, you'd go out into the park again for a while until it was time to get on the bus and come back to Ashton. Sometimes it would be a canal trip to Marple and it would go from Portland Basin. It wasn't a canal barge like they are now, deliberately done up for passenger transport; it would be a canal barge which probably had sand on the floor to cover up where they had been transporting stuff in it. You'd sit round the edges of it, and a horse would pull it to Marple or somewhere like that. It used to pull up at the side of a big field, and there was a Sunday school adjacent to this field. They had obviously booked this Sunday school. We'd have our sandwiches, play in this field, then come

back on this barge at night. Once or twice there were people that fell over the side of the barge before we even set off. I don't know how we managed to book the barges, but they were ordinary barges, used for commercial purposes. Lots of Sunday schools did it. We thought it was a magical trip – the big horse pulling you along. The canal was full of dead dogs and all sorts; it was like that at that time. The highlight was getting enough money off your mother to get a big bottle of pop to take with you and try to make it last. There was always a singsong when we were coming back.

(H.I.)

## Love To Sing, Hate To Dance!

We used to put on pantomimes and things at church. I played Dandini in *Cinderella*

Cinderella *at Henry Square Methodist Church. Joyce Wardle (later Iliffe), seen second from left,* *played Dandini.*

*Whit Walks, c. 1920. Alice Wood is in front, with the crook.*

*Whit Walks, in the early 1940s. Joyce and Grace Wardle on the far side of flower display.*

and I was the prince in something and the king in something else. In the summer we sometimes put on something more like a variety show. We sometimes got asked to do our shows at other places. I remember going to Ryecroft Independent (that was opposite where West End Park is now), and to Charlestown. I used to sing and I enjoyed it, but, when it came to tap-dancing, I had two left feet. I'd master it by the end, but it was uphill work.

(J.I.)

## The Whit Walks

The Whit Walks were always quite well attended; virtually everybody in the church, except a few very old ones, would walk. There was a banner, and there was quite a fuss about getting positioned on a banner cord or a banner ribbon. They used to put a list up and you'd be picked to go on it. There was a definite list of seniority for getting on banner cords or ribbons, and there would be disappointed people. The Bible was always carried by four boys; the basket was carried by girls; then there was a Primary banner, or God's Garden Banner, with all the Primary children behind it. Then the adults, in twos, behind. We started from Henry Square, walked up Old Street directly to the market, back along George Street and back down Stamford Street to Chester Square, past our own church (Henry Square) turn left, go down onto Victoria Street, and come round in a square so that we'd approach the church from the back. Then we had tea and raspberry buns – a very hard bun with a bit of raspberry jam in the centre. Looking back you realise they were very hard, cheap buns, with a

*Whit Walks in the 1950s. Market hall on left, Henrietta Street in background.*

*Whit Walks on the market ground in front of the Town Hall.*

*Children of Henry Square Methodist Church outside the church after the Whit Walks. The street on the right is Welbeck Street; this section has long been demolished.*

little bit of jam on top. But everyone had one; we thought they were marvellous.

(H.I.)

## Carrying the Banner

When we were very young, we all had little baskets of flowers, and they had little banners for us. The boys would carry a Bible with flowers round, or a basket of flowers. Then, when you were fourteen, you got on a banner ribbon, and the older girls were on a banner cord with one of the men. We used to walk up to the market then and assemble there. All the stalls were moved. They put the banners along by the market wall. The market was absolutely full. When we were walking people used to run out into the street and give the walkers money. It was just a custom, like giving money for Whitsun clothes. You used to go round and show people your new clothes and everybody gave you money. If you had a lot of relatives and friends you'd do quite well.

(G.W.)

## Milk and a Raspberry Bun

When we got home, after walking, we used to change into a little cotton dress and pumps and go to the playing fields. We'd go back to Sunday school for milk, always a cup of milk and a raspberry bun.

(A.G.)

# CHAPTER 4

# *War*

*Ashton men in the Fire Service during the Second World War.*

## Zeppelin

During the First War we weren't prepared at all; England weren't prepared; it were thrust on us. I were never afraid, during both wars, never once. I found life as hard as wars. I remember standing at door one night, and I thought, 'What's that roar?' I looked up at the sky and I saw the most beautiful thing I'd ever seen in me whole life. It were the length of the row of houses where I lived. It were every colour. It had come down that low, and it were Zeppelin. Everybody run in and put their lights out. I didn't. I looked up and I thought, 'Ooh, ain't it lovely!' He'd only to have dropped one and we'd all 'a gone.

(E.M)

## Bombs! What Bombs?

I think Ashton had two or three bombs in the duration of the war. One was on the

Moss, I think; one was on Birch Street, at the side of the Birch Hotel. It hit the railway line and bent all the lines. I can remember going and looking at those. I remember picking up shrapnel from the anti-aircraft guns outside the Tin Mission, on what is now Portland Basin Square, on the way to school. I don't think Ashton was affected by the air raids any more than that. Me brother was in a reserved occupation because he was an engineer. At night he became a messenger, and had a steel helmet with an 'M' printed on the front of it in white. They were supposed to take messages between police stations and ARP posts. We used to go across Church Street, when the sirens went, into a house opposite that had a large cellar underneath, two large cellars in fact, and quite a lot of us out of the street used to pile into these two cellars. The children would play in one of them and the adults would sit round in the other. The one thing I remember was hoping against hope that the air raid lasted longer than a certain time at night, because, if it did, you didn't have to go to school in the morning. All the children that were in shelters at that time were desperately hoping that the all-clear wouldn't go till afterwards and then they could stay off school.

(H.I.)

## The Sound of Destruction

I remember one of the girls in the office – I think she was in Stretford – saying that they were in a shelter and a whole row of houses was hit, and it sounded just like a child going with a stick along an iron fencing.

(I.S.)

## The Birch Street Bomb

We used to spend quite a lot of time walking around the streets looking for shrapnel. It was better than gold when you found a piece of shrapnel. We got our fingers burned once or twice because the shrapnel was still hot when we tried to pick it up. The nearest bomb to us that fell was on Birch Street; y'know, the Birch Hotel where Birch Street goes over the railway. A bomb dropped there just at the side of the railway, no more than four or five feet from the line. It was very useful to us the following year and thereafter, because we could collect tadpoles in this brand new pond. We'd been to Belle Vue once and a thunderstorm came on and we took shelter. The lightning was striking the barrage balloons and bringing them down on fire. Me mother was terrified but I thought it was marvellous.

(A.B.)

## A Rude Awakening

I remember all going into the cellar on Oldham Road. My dad, he never used to bother. He got in bed; he'd never get out of it. Once he got blown out of bed with a bomb that dropped across the way, across the other side of Oldham Road. We saw this big crater and we used to go looking for shrapnel. But my dad never went down that cellar. He said, typically, 'Bugger it!'

(D.F.)

## The Night They Bombed Manchester

I remember the first day of the war. They

said it was imminent and we all gathered round the radio, and this voice came over saying that unless the German army was withdrawn from Poland, war would start. I remember the first sirens going. I was alone with Paul and I grabbed him out of his bed and came and hid under the stairs. Every night at 10.30 the bombers came over. The fellow next door was a builder and he dug a dugout in the garden and he put bunk beds in and we took the children out of bed at half past ten every night and went down into this thing and put the kids to sleep again. We got so fed up after a while that we said, 'Oh, this is no use'. So we brought the beds downstairs and slept in the lounge. The night they bombed Manchester was Paul's first birthday – December 21 1940. We were all there having a party, and it was so bad, the bombs were so bad, that no-one could go home. They slept anywhere, on the floor, on the settee, anywhere. Mext morning it was so icy that no-one could stand on their feet. It was just like a sheet of glass. And Manchester had gone. You could see the glow in the sky. It was terrible, terrible.

(A.G.)

## Husband & Wife Killed

### Plane Crashes After Unloading Bombs

Two or three persons were killed, including a man and his wife, and a number were injured when bombs demolished houses in an industrial area of a north-west town on Wednesday night.

It is believed that the plane which caused the damage had been hit by antiaircraft fire, and that it unloaded its bombs to gain height, but it crashed a few miles away.

Mr. and Mrs. Ernest Dawson, whose house was demolished, died from their injuries.

A number of people were injured and taken to hospital. The majority were suffering from shock and cuts from flying glass, but a number were detained.

A public house had its frontage damaged, and many windows were broken.

Civil defence workers, rescue squads and neighbours worked feverishly to extricate the people buried in the wreckage of their own homes. All were got out quickly and rushed to hospital for treatment.

The police headed the civil defence workers, who all worked valiantly and strenuously, ambulances being quickly on the spot to deal with the wounded. There were some remarkable escapes.

*An article from Ashton-under-Lyne Reporter, 9 May 1941, about the Hillgate bombing. Note that the name of the town is not given.*

## Holding The Ceiling Up

Two streets away from Egerton Street was a mill, a cotton mill. A bomb dropped on it. It didn't damage our houses, but all the windows in me Gran's house were knocked in. I clearly remember me mother wrapping me up on the bed, and me dad was standing on the bed – me dad was very, very tall – and he was trying to hold the ceiling up. The noise was tremendous, 'cos it was only round the corner; the mill was on Mount Pleasant Street.

(E.B.)

## Hillgate

I was working at the Assistance Board, a big house on Currier Lane. There was a bomb dropped on Ashton, in Hillgate. There was one boy killed there, an eighteen-year-old boy. It was very sad to see the people at the Assistance Board the following morning. They had to come in just what clothes they could borrow. But we were able to give them some money to fit them up for the time being.

(I.S.)

## Collapsible Air Raid Shelters

They built us some air raid shelters. One day my father-in-law had been having a smoke at the door. He came in and said, 'Mr Bowden wants to borrow a prop'. So I went to get it out of the back yard. He took it to Mr Bowden and he was trying the wall of this air raid shelter and it fell down. So they were never used. Wouldn't have been much use, would they?

(Mrs A.B.)

## Running To The Air Raid Shelter

We got to the shelter once and there were this young woman from round the corner. I were dressed in no time, but I got ready night before, chance he'd come, but she wouldn't bother. She'd come running with corsets under her arm and her nightdress on and nowt on her feet. 'Ooh, I am feared', she says. 'Aye, but I bet you stopped in bed right t' last minute'.

(E.M.)

## A Miserable Safety

We had air raid shelters in the back garden. People came along and dug a big hole and stuck this like corrugated iron in it. It had a sump in the corner and that used to get full of water and you used to have to bale it out before you could go in the shelter. It must have been very wet and miserable, but, when the sirens went, you just went out and you huddled in this shelter.

(H.F.)

## 'I'm Not Going In There Again'

They built air raid shelters on Church Street, just round the corner from Margaret Street where we lived. The lady next door but one to us made one of them comfortable for her family. But me mother only went in one night and she said, 'I'm not going in there again'. It was freezing cold and we used to go and sit on the cellar steps; but the coal was in the cellar. It's a wonder we weren't black. I remember going to school one day and everybody was talking about this bomb which had been dropped on Birch Street. We only lived on Margaret Street and we didn't know anything about it. We'd slept through it. Me mother said if we were going to die; we'd die in our beds.

(G.W.)

## Hartshead Pike and the Home Guard

During the Second World War my father slept in Hartshead Pike to guard it. He was on duty in the Home Guard up there. He slept inside the Pike. They had a little sweetshop inside the Pike then, where they sold sweets and things. Part of the Home Guard's duty was to guard the beacon.

(H.F.)

Left: *Hartshead Pike, 1938. The windows have long been bricked up.* Right: *A wartime ration book.*

## Rationing

You had two eggs a week and you could either have a pound of jam or a pound of sugar. You couldn't have both. You had 2oz butter and 2oz bacon for each ration book. So the bigger your family the better you did. And the meat … what you see in *Dad's Army* is absolutely true. 'You can have one sausage'.

(A.G.)

## Queuing for Sweets

I remember having two ounces of butter and so much sugar. If there were any sweets on Stamford Street, at the shop on Stamford Street, there used to be a queue a mile long.

(D.S.)

## Handouts

My brother, who by then was married, worked at Alan Shaw's, at the beginning of the Avenue. So we got bits of handouts. You used your ration book, but he gave you a bit more. That used to be a good shop. They used to give you a bit of cheese, to try it.

(Mrs E.C.)

## Liquid Corned Beef

When we bumped into the Yanks in Burma we made friends with one or two on the train. We were sometimes on the train two or three days. A Yank opened his emergency rations and I opened mine. Mine were a tin of bully beef and some thick biscuits; he had a little bit of dried egg and a bit of something else. 'D' you want to change?' he said. 'Aye', I said. He preferred mine. With it being a hot climate the corned beef were … well, you could pour it out. But he enjoyed it, and I enjoyed his, 'cos it were a change, weren't it?

(N.B.)

## Gas Masks

I carried a gas mask. You had to carry one and y'had to take it to school with you. It was in a cardboard box. If you were a bit posh, you had it in a little canvas box. You had a string over your shoulder. Babies had a gas-mask. It was a huge thing. They put the whole baby in. Like a space helmet. Then there was something called 'Mickey Mouse'; It had a thing on the nose. They were for smaller kids, three or four years old. The baby's gas mask had a bellows on the side that you pumped.

(B.N.)

## A Boy's Memory of War

I know we had blackouts. The air raid warden came round one night because we were showing a light through the kitchen. He came a'playing hell. I remember the bombs being dropped on Hillgate, and then the flying bombs came over, and a couple dropped up Oldham somewhere. We used to read the paper and each morning it would show you how far they'd advanced in Germany or Italy or wherever they were. They'd show you different pictures of aeroplanes – 'Watch for this German

coming over'. I remember a spitfire coming over Lees Road one morning. He was so low you could see the pilot. It was just skimming the trees.

(B.P.)

## Ack-ack in the Morning

One morning there was this plane – you could see it from our back door; it came up over Hurst Cross, about 7.50 in the morning. They opened fire on it; there was an ack-ack battery at Littlemoss. I remember them opening fire. They say that one was finally brought down at Huddersfield.

(B.N.)

## An Encounter Far From Home

I were in Calcutta, in a long, narrow restaurant. I were sitting down with my mates. There's four or five more soldiers a bit further down on the right hand side. I saw the back of this lad's head and I thought, 'There's only one. It's got to be him'. It were; it were Timmy Edwards. I said, 'Timmy, bloody hell!' That night, walking around Calcutta, I bet I bumped into him three or four times. Then, after that, I never saw him again up to coming home after the war. I still see him; he's still knocking around.

(N.B.)

## Bren Gun Carriers and POWs

Some soldiers were killed on Lees Road in a bren gun carrier. Where Hartshead School is, there was a long field. They used to practise driving in that field, these bren gun carriers. This one had gone through the wall on Lees Road and about four of them were killed. They used to race up and down Lees Road on those bren gun carriers. There were hundreds of German prisoners in Ashton. Whittaker's Mill, which was off Queen's Road, was where they all were – army, air force, Luftwaffe, even sailors. It was full of them, and Italians. In fact, when things relaxed a bit, they used to walk out. They had orange patches on their back. I can see them now, when I was at Stamford School, marching them up to the barracks.

(B.N.)

## Letters from the Cellar

Round the corner [from where we lived] was the brush works. When the war started, they had a cellar we could go in when the sirens went. One Sunday night, down in the cellar, Jim Hall said to me, 'I must write to Ernie this week'. I said, 'Why? Have you got his address?' He said he had. So I said, 'I'll write to him', not thinking anything, only as friends. So down in that cellar, I wrote letters to Ernie.

(Mrs E.C.)
*(Note: Mrs Copeland has been married to Ernie now for more than fifty-four years)*

## Casualties of War

I remember going to the pictures one night. We came home and one of me dad's brothers had been to tell him that one of his younger brothers had been killed, in Burma. I remember coming in and me mother and dad were all upset. Me mother's cousin, we got a letter from him on November 4th; he wrote it on the 2nd.

*Outside Whittaker's Mill. The carrier is Mr James Parkinson.*

They must have taken the mail off his boat and the boat had been blown up. He was actually dead when we got his letter, but we didn't know. He was only ever, 'Missing; presumed killed', because there were no bodies.

(G.W.)

## Food Parcels and Firewatchers' Dances

During the war we had a firewatchers' scheme. We had the ladders at the side of our house; we were in charge of the ladders and the buckets. My father fixed up some things to hang them by the side of our house. The neighbours used to have little tea parties or supper parties or potato pie suppers. They charged for these and then they sent parcels to those who had gone into the forces. We also used to have Firewatchers' dances.

(H.F.)

## Dinner at the Baths

During the war you could buy a meal at the baths. At lunchtime you would go to the front of the baths and get your ticket; then you came round to the back of the baths – you can still see the doorway there in the old building – and handed your tickets in and you got a main course and a sweet, depending on what tickets you'd bought. If you could afford to do this a couple of times a week, you got two cooked meals that were in addition to your rations, because you didn't have to present any ration coupons. You took your own pots and they put it in your pots. You could, if you were a worker, go in the baths at the front and pay. There

*A Christmas card sent to Grace Wardle's family by her cousin from his ship, during the Second World War.*

was a canteen inside and you could actually eat the meal inside the baths.

(H.I.)

## A Soldier's Return

One Saturday morning me mother got this telegram – 'Arrived safely. Home Saturday or Sunday'. Me dad came home from Italy in a Lancaster. He said they were just piled in; all the seats were taken out and they just sat on the floor. He landed at Peterborough, came up on the train Saturday morning and got off at Guide Bridge station. He got on a bus then to come to Ashton, in all his rig-out, and the bus conductress wouldn't take his fare off him. After tea, all the aunts and uncles gathered at our house. It was early evening when he

*Elsie Brown's dad.*

arrived. He was enormous; he was tall and brown. Everybody was sat in that room crying. Next morning he took me for a walk down to the stable. When all these soldiers were coming home and the airmen, everybody put flags out and bunting. We got out of our house and I said, 'All these flags are for you'. It must have been strange for the men really, because they were coming back to wives they hadn't seen for five years. Towards the end of the war, when the Red Cross went to all these places, the soldiers were allowed to make a record to send home to their family. Me dad had been home weeks when his record arrived. Then everybody was crying again at this record.

(E.B.)

## Home on Leave

When a soldier came home on leave anywhere in our street, everybody used to

*Ashton Baths. The building, long closed, is still there.*

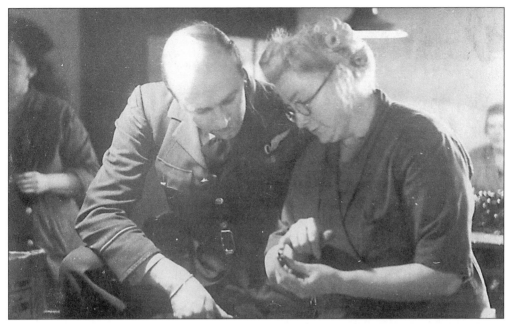

*Mrs Annie Burgum, mother of Annie Armitage, explaining her war work to an RAF officer.*

contribute to his tea or to a cake. People used to find a bit of sugar, or an egg, a bit of tea or something. The soldiers were like gods coming back from the war, and they were treated as such, as far as people could.

(A.B.)

## Observing Armistice Day

I also remember, from my schooldays in the late 1920s, what was then known as Armistice Day, because of the solemnness. The day was treated with such solemnity. [We would hear] the maroons in Ashton, which denoted the start of the two-minute silence.

(J.M.)

*An airgraph sent to Mrs Ethel Parkinson by a relative serving in Greece, Christmas 1944.*

73

# CHAPTER 5

## Shopping

*Ashton Market, c. 1910.*

### Ashton Market in the 1920s

They sold practically everything on different stalls, and in[side] the market as well. There were little open eating houses in market, and you could go in, or sit just outside and you could have a cuppa tea or cakes and ham sandwiches. This were very nice when you went shopping … and [there were] plenty of ice-cream carts. On the market you could get anything from a pin to a house of furniture. Monday were the real shopping day. Seen many a scrap with the women, when they've had a couple of cutties. They've come out and they've been fighting on the market before today, when I were younger. Never bothered. Best of friends when they met again.

(E.M.)

## Ashton Market on a Winter Night

In winter they lit up these acetylene lanterns, up above the market stalls. They were a particularly big lantern and they used to hiss. You had the toffee stall, Podmore's, and Bates and Marsh, who used to have their pot auctions, and the people who came from Wem, in Shropshire, to bring cheeses. The whole thing was fascinating, Ashton market on a dark night, lit by lamps.

(J.M.)

## The Market – Smashing!

There were the fruit stalls, and Podmore's the sweets. Then somebody used to come on with chocolates –good chocolates. Then there were Fish, selling oilcloth and carpets. And somebody selling pots. Ooh! It was smashing!

(A.A.)

## Stamford Street in the 1920s

Next to the Wine Lodge was Seymour Meads, a grocer's. They put your money in a thing and it went whizzing across the shop. There was Harrop's herbalist further down, facing the Avenue. At the corner of Warrington Street was Howarth's. Then there was a gents' outfitter – don't remember his name – then it was Woolworths. Then,

Stamford Street in the 1930s.

*An advertisement for Leigh and Ardern's.*

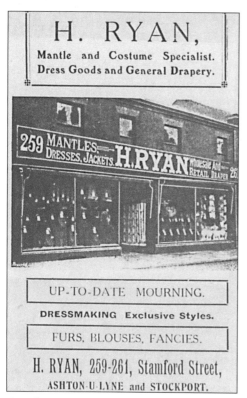

*An advertisement for Ryan's.*

of course, there's the arcade, the old arcade and a bank on the corner. Then it was Pike's and Littlewoods. Opposite there was Arnold's a very nice furniture shop. It was 'the' shop for furniture. Next door to the Wesleyan Methodist church was the Lounge Café – that was very posh – and I think there was a furniture shop on the corner. Then there was Freeman, Hardy and Willis' shoe shop, facing the Methodist church higher up. Radcliffe's confectioners, Lindley's confectioners, Roebuck's and Ryan's Ladies Outfitters near Cavendish Street. And there was Benson's Pork shop.

(Mrs A.B.)

## Stamford Street Before the Second World War

There were all sorts of shops. There was Newbert's; they sold things like bedding and tablecloths; and Leigh and Ardern's, who used to do soft furnishings. There was a very nice ladies' outfitters called Ryans. It was between Henry Square and Cavendish Street. On the opposite side of the road was a leather shop; I think they used to make their own leather goods. Nearer to Henry Square was a shop where you could buy a lot of 'seconds' materials that were very much cheaper than you could buy in other shops. The schoolteacher, when we were going to make a dress at school, said, 'Tell your mother she can get material at Roebuck's for 4d a yard'. Originally Spencer's bookshop was lower down Stamford Street, on the corner of one of those streets; it might have been Oldham Road because Oldham Road came down and across Stamford Street. Pollard's the stationer's was on Stamford Street for a long time. There was a shop called Howard's, on the corner of Stamford Street and Warrington Street. Woolworth's used to be there. Then there was the Clarence Arcade. And one of the shops on there, a big shop, was where they sold pianos and gramophones and records.

(I.S.)

*An advertisement for Marchington's*

that. I think it was at the bottom of Stamford Street. Spencer's bookshop used to be down there as well, before it moved.

## Mason's, Marchington's and Spencer's Bookshop

My mum used to do all her shopping in Mason's, which was just facing Stamford Street Methodist church. It was in that little row there. She got her groceries and things from there. We used to shop on the market for vegetables and things like that. Marchington's was a haberdashery, where they sold materials, silks and things like

## Stamford Street 'Was' Ashton

Spencers had a small bookshop on Stamford Street. We used to go there for stamps. All the kids were collecting stamps and we used to go there and buy these packets of 'French Colonials'. Stamford Street was the main street of Ashton – Stamford Street was Ashton. Y'had all the shops round there – Bower's, the leather shop (shop's still there, but long, long closed; it had a little balcony

*The bottom end of Stamford Street, c. 1906. The baths and St Peter's church can be clearly seen.*

on the top there – I don't know what they used it for). The main jeweller's, of course, was Kenworthy's; everybody used to go there for their engagement rings. We had Woolworths, and Littlewoods, which is now Hitchen's, There was Roebuck's, Leigh and Ardern's, quite a lot of big shops. Lot of tailors. Vincent's piano shop – we used to go there for sheet music, because you didn't buy the record; you had to go and get the music to learn the words. You'd buy some sheet music there at Vincent's. It was at the bottom end of Stamford Street, well below Arcadia.

(J.E.)

## Shopping Heaven on Stamford Street

In the first block of Stamford Street was an outfitters called Roebuck's, quite a big one. They sold all kinds of clothes, gloves and all kinds of haberdashery like that. They had the old system where they had a cashier in a box and they screwed little pots onto wires and shot them across the shop, which fascinated me as a child. One of the things which me mother always said, and I've never had any evidence to prove this, 'Oh, you don't shop at Roebuck's; all their stuff is shop-rotten; it falls to pieces when you get it home'. It was obvious something my mother had got from there at one time had fallen to pieces and so the shop was forever damned. Further up was Arcadia, with its grocer's; it had household stuff, carpets, men's and women's wear, the bank upstairs and a café. There were radio shops and bike shops. There was a tiny shop near the traffic lights on Stamford Street, near the Arcadia corner. It was a tiny shop that you went in if you wanted to buy the latest record. It was one room, one tiny room,

*The top end of Stamford Street in the 1940s.*

*Mrs Gertrude Iliffe, Harry's mum, who liked a man to wear 'a blue serge suit and a white shirt', is on the extreme left of this group of pretty ladies.*

with another tiny room behind it. The records were all stacked behind the counter, and you would ask the woman, 'Have you got a copy of?' what was the favourite of the day. She would fumble in the racks at the back. Then, of course, there was the 35s tailor's and the 50s tailor's, and, if you were really posh, there was Burton's in the top block. Burton's was at the side of the Wine Lodge. I think it was the 50s tailor's [where] I had my first suit made. It was quite an experience to go in and be measured for a suit, and pick from a load of little bits of cloth which material you fancy, and then hope, when you got back home with that suit, that mother wouldn't say, 'What did you buy that for?' Mother firmly believed that men only looked nice in blue serge with a nice white shirt and a very stiff collar. I must have done all right because I never got any complaint. There was a herbalist you could go in and buy a drink. Quite a lot of people used to go in there on the way home from the mills, regularly once a week, and have a drink of some herb or other that was supposed to do something magical for them for the rest of the week. I won't go into what it was supposed to do, but these herbs kept you healthy in different ways, and quite a few people on a Friday night on the way home from work called in for a glass of whatever. Of course there was Woolies up there. It had a wooden floor. It was the only shop that I can remember in Ashton that had a woodblock floor. I remember that it creaked and when you got a lot of people walking through on a Saturday afternoon you could really hear Woolworths creaking. It's also the shop where I remember getting most of my Christmas presents from, because it was the kind of toys that me mother could afford, the kind that were sold in Woolworths.

(H.I.)

## Saturday Afternoon on Stamford Street

Stamford Street used to be thronged with people on a Saturday afternoon. If you were to stand on Henry Square about two o'clock on a Saturday afternoon, then all the people would be streaming up from down the West End, Trafalgar Square way and that. They'd go up Stamford Street, through the Avenue at the top, across onto the market and in the market, and back down Old Street, because there were still quite a number of shops on Old Street at that time, back to Henry Square and back home from there. Presumably the same thing happened with people coming down from the Hurst area into Ashton on a Saturday, the same with Smallshaw.

(H.I.)

## The Building of Arcadia

I was born at 155 Old Street on August 6 1922. My parents kept a sweetshop, opposite the library. One of the memories I have is in 1926 they built Arcadia. To build Arcadia they knocked down a row of six shops on Stamford Street. It opened in 1927. On the side next to the pub, that was originally a grocer's. The chemist shop was at the opposite end of the front from the grocer's On the top floor were offices. The ground floor and the basement there was furniture. I can also remember an electrical section with gramophones and radios.

(H.K.)

## A Bit Old-Fashioned

Arcadia was a bit old-fashioned. They used to have the money go into things that shot across the shop. Arcadia had their own bank and everything upstairs. They had their own furniture department; the furniture was quite good there. They had a grocer's next to it. Then they sold fancy goods and clothes; they sold everything. Arcadia belonged to the Co-op. Then there was the Co-op shop at the top of Stamford Street: that sold mostly glass and china. The assistants all seemed to be from the church we go to now, which was then Trafalgar Square – Ada and Leah, the two Yeoman sisters, and Annie Armitage.

(G.W.)

## The Avenue

The Avenue, that was very nice. There was a lovely shop called Walker's, where they roasted their coffee. The smell was lovely when you walked down the Avenue. There were lots of different shops on either side. There was another shop called Burrows', which sold tea. My mother used to like to buy tea from Burrows'. Then there was Lumb's toyshop. And Burgess and Dyson, the bookshop, was on there.

(I.S.)

An advertisement for Arcadia.

## Calling on Miss Hill

My mother used to work in the Avenue, at Miss Hill's. We always used to call there, because Miss Hill, who owned the shop, always wanted to see us as we were growing up. The Avenue was fascinating. There was the smell of Walker's ground coffee in their shop there.

(J.M.)

## Nice Toyshops

[There were] nice toyshops on the Avenue, Bowers' and Gibson's and places like that. I

81

think Gibson's is still there, near the market end. They used to sell Dinky toys there, motor cars. Bowers' was a handbag shop, just a little bit further down. It was mainly toys in those days and other gifts. There was a bookshop next to it.

(A.B.)

## The Indoor Market

Part of the indoor market was a fish market; and another part of it was the electricity showroom. If you stand on Town Hall steps and look to your left, there's some arches. That was the fish market and after that it was the electricity showroom.

(B.N.)

## Tom Tweed, The Butcher

There was a butcher's shop next to Henry Moon's called Tom Tweed. The butcher's shop where mother used to go, if she could, was Harry Stenton's, on Curzon Road, top end there. I don't think it's a butcher's shop now. But mother used to say to me, 'I think you'd better go to Tom Tweed's for the mince this week. It's half a penny cheaper'. So I used to walk down to Tom Tweed's for half a pound of mince, because it was half a penny cheaper there.

(D.J.)

## Hayward's The Chippy

On Sundays you were not allowed to buy chips, but one firm on Katherine Street,

Hayward's, used to save all the small potatoes and do them on a Sunday. There was big queues because they used to put potatoes in hot fat, not chips. So they didn't break the regulations on a Sunday night. I think it might have been on Warrington Street. There were various shops there – old clock shops, pawnbrokers (gilded balls and the smell of old clothes if you went in the pawnbrokers for something). I think one of them was Sizer's, a pawnbroking firm. My father used to do work for them, so I would visit at times.

(J.M.)

## Jones' Music Shop

Jones' music shop faced the market. Phil Jones, who had the shop there, was a friend of my friend's mother. We used to go to the music shop a lot, and Jean [my friend] had a little job there. When we were at school, she used to go on Saturday afternoons, and I used to go down on a Saturday and go into the music shop and we played records and listened to them. Then there was a milk bar a little further along, just past the Avenue, and we used to meet in there after school, when we were old enough to be going into Ashton.

(H.F.)

## Polly's Tripe Stall

I remember Polly's tripe stall; she had a tripe stall on the corner of Bow Street and Market Street. Polly and her brother also had a shop on Mill Lane. Mill Lane used to

An advertisement for Jones' music shop.

An advertisement for Howard's milk bar.

*The Grey Horse pub on Oldham Road. The men are assembling for a trip. The licensee, Mr Christopher Naden, and his wife, can be seen in the doorway.*

lead down to the old water mill. Polly had another tripe shop there.

(H.K.)

## Pot Stalls and Eating Houses

Me mother could remember the shops opening very late. She could remember the butchers having thrupenny parcels of meat, selling it up because they didn't have fridges. People used to go up to Ashton late. Then there were the pot stalls on the market. They used to be open very late. My mother used to talk about eating houses – they mustn't have called them cafés then. They all made pies, and peas and chips and things, and people went in there and had something to eat. Saturday night that was what my mother did. Her mother didn't get out; so Saturday night they went up and got meat and went round. Me grandma was very fond of these pot stalls; she was always buying bits and pieces. Then they'd go in one of these eating houses and have some food.

(G.W.)

## Shopping on Oldham Road

Oldham Road's never been changed for years. There was the greengrocer's, then the baker's; there was a newsagent's, a chip shop, the haberdashery shop, all in the same block. Jubbs, the baker's, has stayed the same all the time. The Jubb family's been there all my life, different generations. You can tell Jubbs' because it's never been painted for donkey's years. They're always glad to see me when I go in. I only go in once a week and get me eggs and bread. They're two brothers, and their parents had the shop before them. They have carried on the tradition. It's very good bread, the best I have anywhere.

*(D.F.)*

## My Own Florist Shop

I had me own shop. After I left the Co-op, Waterloo Co-op, for the second time, I opened a little shop facing Dog pub, Dog and Partridge. I took a course on floristry, making wreaths and wedding things and whatnot. There were a little run down shop – it used to be a tripe shop when I were going to school – and it weren't doing much. I thought, 'He'll not reign long there'. So I opened it up and I had four good years there, doing weddings and green grocery and so forth. I had name put on – 'Buckley's greengrocers and florists'. Then Asda came and I thought, 'That's going to ruin the village', and it did.

*(N.B.)*

*Hurst Cross, c. 1910.*

## Hurst Cross

At Hurst Cross there was a toffee shop called Jessie Lees', where we all went for toffees. Next to it was a butcher's shop. Across the way was May Bailey's, a wet-fish shop; then two more houses; then a chip shop, which my granny owned then, 1944, during war time. Then it was another mixed business, then Ogden Street, two more houses and the Royal Oak. Across the way from there, which is the bottom of Kenworthy Avenue, was another mixed business, then about six houses, and the newspaper shop. There used to be a Victorian cast iron and glass bus shelter at Hurst Cross, which everybody played in, and often broke the glass. There was a policeman around Hurst Cross, Bobby Long, who used to look after things.

*Granny Parkinson, who had a fish shop at Hurst Cross.*

(B.P.)

*Stockport Road. Oxford Park is on the left.*

## The Shops of Stockport Road

Stockport Road was a little hive of industry. People didn't go into Ashton, you see; they shopped there. At the bottom of Birch Street there was a lovely butcher's; next door to him was Leonard Hartley, the grocer – absolutely high-class grocer – it was a huge shop, known all over. Higher up, on the other side, was a lovely confectioner's. Where the garage is now, that was Froggatt's. There was a shop on the corner of Birch Street and you had to go up steps to it, about eight stone steps. On the opposite corner was a bootmender's; you had to duck down to go in; it was just like a square in the wall, where he worked. You climbed in there to talk to him or to take your shoes to be mended. Then, higher up, there was a lovely confectioner's, and a few houses before you came to the other shops - a tripe shop, a greengrocer's, and a hairdresser's.

(A.G.)

## Grandma's Tripe Shop

When I was a child in the 1920s the area of Stockport Road between Trafalgar Square and West End Park was crowded with shops, on both sides of the road. My grandmother, Mrs Martha Naden, had a tripe shop on Stockport Road, in the block between Cambridge Street and Cecil Street. Next door was Jessie's Tuck shop, then Judson's fishmongers, Gregory's meat shop, Barnes' haberdashery and a pawnshop. Then there was Cecil Street. The Pinapple Inn (still there, but derelict) was across Cecil Street, and next to it was Lingard's confectioner's. Mrs Lingard made the raspberry buns that we had at church after the Whit Walks. On the other side of the road, in the first block from Trafalgar Square, you had Boardman's Fancy Goods, Carpets and Rugs; then there was Whiteland's newspaper shop; next door was Clifford's shoe shop, then Thompson's grocer's. Then there was a chemist called

*Stockport Road, looking from Trafalgar Square towards Chester Square.*

*Mrs Martha Naden with her son, Robert, and daughter, Ruth.*

Butterworth, a signwriter, a wool shop, and Norton's butcher's shop. Then, after Grosvenor Street, you had Mary's, Carter's toffee shop, a tripe shop, Peet's the newspaper shop, Ashton's confectioner's, a shoe shop, another sweet shop and the Co-op chemist. My 'Aunty' Polly had the sweet shop, and she used to put on the counter two boxes – a penny box and a halfpenny box. These were divided into sections, and the children could take their pick for a penny or a halfpenny.

(M.L.)

## The Shops of Margaret Street

I remember the shops on Margaret Street, and playing in the light of the shops at night. There was a shop opposite [our house] called Allcock's, a mixed grocery. There was a similar one on the next row, Bowden's, and there was a newsagent on there. Joined onto our house was Dewsnap's grocer's shop; he ground his own coffee. On the other side was Draycott's, a draper's, who sold absolutely everything. Then there was Bailey's; they cooked their own meat and made brawn and stuff like that. There was a pie shop at the bottom, a lovely confectioner's. Then on Victoria Street – that was at the bottom of Margaret Street – there was a row of shops – a newsagent's, a grocer's-cum-greengrocer's called Percy Hill's, and a barber, Ira Gee, all the lads went to for their haircuts. Then there was a lady called Mrs Bullock, who had a draper's shop; she was also a dressmaker and we used to go and buy our own material and she made the clothes. Then there was a butcher's and a little sweet shop. There were chip shops everywhere; there was one near where we lived on Margaret Street – Mr Oldfield's chip shop; he always let us have the first lot out, – and there were two or three on Victoria Street.

(G.W.)

## Working in Roebuck's in 1937

My friend Thelma said, 'There's a job going at Roebuck's. D'you want to come?' So I went there, and I worked on the back counter downstairs, the Manchester counter. As you went into Roebuck's there was a tiny kiosk, with children's socks; then came menswear, and a long hosiery counter. In the middle of the shop were fabrics. Drapery, pillow cases and net

*An advertisement for Roebuck's.*

# E. Roebuck & Co.

Newest
Creations
and
Smart
Novelties
in every
department.

**The Fashionable Drapers.**

A
Visit
of
Inspection
respectfully
invited.

## 279, 281, 283, 285, STAMFORD STREET.

Telephone 538.

All parcels carriage free.

*Roebuck's staff at their annual dance.*

*Church Street.*

curtains were on the Manchester counter. Upstairs were ladies' dresses. There was also a little room where we did pressing of garments, and there were some changing rooms. When the customer paid, the money was put into a little pot, the assistant pulled on a wire and the pot whizzed across the shop to the cashier. Norman Leech was first salesman on the Manchester counter and Dolly Gordon were second; being the junior I was third sales. Each department dressed its own window, and I used to help with ours. The manager was Mr Wright. Being the youngest member of staff, I used to brew his tea. He used to be thrilled to bits if your parents came in. Roebuck's had a house on Fleet Street where we used to have our meals. Every year they held a staff dance at a hotel in Manchester.

(A.A.)

## Street Vendors and Singers

Different people would come around the streets selling things. There would be people selling greens because there was a firm in Ashton, somewhere up Oldham Road, called Frost's, that rented out handcarts. I think it cost something like 2s 6d a day to rent a handcart. The renter would take it on Ashton Moss, get salad greens from one of the market gardens, and take them round the streets, selling them. A chap came down the street now and again with a bicycle with a grindstone on; he used to grind all the kitchen knives. Sometimes, on a Sunday afternoon, there would be street-singers who came down; these were people that had a very good voice, but probably only knew one song. They came down and sang it, and hoped people would throw pennies. When they'd got enough pennies for a pint, they went round the corner into the nearest pub and spent them. Sometimes down the street would come this man with a little cart of his own, and he used to bring around black peas in a container. People would take out a basin and I think it was tuppence a basin for black peas. I remember my uncle, who lived in the same street, going out with the large jug out of a bedroom set, and asking the man to put his two pennyworth of black peas in there, much to his consternation.

(H.I.)

# CHAPTER 6
# *Work*

*An advertisement for Siddall's ice-cream.*

## Mr Brimelow, The Herbalist

During the First World War we lived quite near the market. I used to go on the market, helping them out, doing little things – 'Can I wrap this? Can I do this?' – just to earn a bob or two to give me mum to help us. Me mum used to get chest medicine off Mr Brimelow, a herbalist. She says, 'Could you find our May a little job, Monday, when she's finished school, and Saturday?' 'Of course I can', he says. So I worked for Mr Brimelow Mondays and Saturdays. Well-known man in Ashton, Mr Brimelow. He'd opened a clinic somewhere on Stockport Road. He used to come on the market.

(M.W.)

## The Smallpox Hospital

Just lower down than Hartshead Pike, this side of the pike, we had a smallpox hospital. It was like a corrugated iron building. It was called the smallpox hospital, so, when that happened in Hurst, they must have taken them there.

(B.P.)

## Ice-Cream Boy

Next door to the foundry was an ice-cream maker – Siddall. They sold award-winning ice cream. For a time my father used to work for them, selling ice cream. He used to have a little pushcart that he took around the streets with ice cream in. They had pushcarts or horses and carts. Later on, when I got near to school-leaving age, I used to work for the ice cream firm on a Saturday. They put the stalls – trailers, as they called them – on Ashton market; they had three there. I used to take stuff up, set them up and then come back to the ice-cream place and do cleaning and filling-up for the rest of the day. When it was all over, I'd go up to the market again, and bring the trailers back and park them in the garage. I used to go there at seven thirty in the morning and, of course, the shops in Ashton didn't close till six o'clock then on a Saturday. So you didn't start bringing the trailers back till about that time and it was more or less seven o'clock Saturday night when I finished. Me wage started off at one shilling a day for that. It went up a bit; I think I got 1s 6d eventually. I used to go on the market ground and we set the trailers up; the women that sold the ice cream used to arrive later. On the side of the market there used to be a café called Howards'. They also made ice cream and sold it on the market. They were a rival firm. All the ladies who worked at our three stalls used to send me to the café to get coffee and tea and toast for them through the day. Of course, they used to buy me a drink and toast. Quite often, at the end of the day, one of them would give me threepence or sixpence for doing it. So I got a bonus on top of my 1s 6d a day.

(H.I)

## Fetching the Meat

Potts butchers had a slaughterhouse near our pen, just round the corner, facing where Atlas Mill was. If he wanted us, he had a whistle for us, and me mam would say, 'You're wanted', and whoever was in would go; our Fred, me, Harold or James would go. He might want some tripe bringing up from pen, fresh tripe, y'see; they cleaned their own tripe. Or he might have bought a couple of heifers and half dozen sheep, and we used to take them down Newmarket Road there, facing Taunton Sunday School. They used to go in a pen there for grazing, till he wanted them. Then he used to say, 'Go down there and bring them up'. Never no pay. Only pay we'd get a sheep's head or a pig's bladder, something like that. I've seen when there's been fog and instead of arriving at Ashton Goods Yard about three o'clock in th'afternoon, it would be nine and ten o'clock at night. We used to get lamps out when it got late, oil lamps, and go down to station. We used to think we were duty bound. And no pay, only a pig's head, or a pig's bladder or a pig's belly!

(N.B.)

*Miss Ruth Naden.*

## A Shattering Surprise

My grandma had a tripe shop – Naden's – and my mother, Ruth, helped her in the shop. On the opposite side of Stockport Road was another tripe shop – Jackson's. When the Jacksons went on holiday, my mother used to look after their shop. On the day in 1917, when there was a terrible explosion in the West End, my mother was serving in the Jackson's tripe shop. The explosion blew her from the shop into the house at the back. She often told me about this.

(M.L.)

## The Thirteen-Year-Old Mill Girl

I went to work proper full time at thirteen. I were up, at thirteen year old, at quarter to five in the morning while half past five at night. We started at eight o'clock. I walked from Winter Street right up, snow and all sorts. There were trams, but everybody couldn't afford a penny or tuppence to go on the tram. And when we were going to work in t'morning, you'd think it were a scholars' walk; there were that many all going t'mill, walking with shawls, clogs. I had a shawl; I thought I were everyone when I got a shawl and a big safety pin, and a box with me breakfast in. I had an illness in Ring Spinning. Well, I went from playing in t'street up to 80 degrees in the Spinning Room. I got what they called 'mill fever' and I collapsed. I'd never been ill from being born.

(E.M.)

## The Knocker-Up

When the mills were going and people had to get up early, a fellow came round with a long bamboo pole and he tapped on your window and he waited until you came and opened the curtains. Five o'clock in the morning he used to come. He got paid for it, of course. He'd come every morning and tap, tap, tap with this flexible pole.

(A.G.)

## Nearly Landlady to Morecambe and Wise

I used to take lodgers in, theatricals. Morecambe and Wise came to the door one week. It was the one week in the month I didn't take anybody in because I got a lady to come and help me clean thoroughly. I didn't know they were Morecambe and Wise. Eric Morecambe looked and he said, 'It looks nice and cosy; we would love to stay'. He asked, 'How much do you charge for full board?' '£3 10s', I says. 'Oh', he says, 'we can't afford that. We only pay 25s in money, and we buy all our own food and you cook it. We don't have full board'. Later they became famous. Then I had Dorothy Squires stay with me. She was very, very nice, but she had a foul mouth. 'Ooh, I don't like you swearing like that,' I said. Then I went through into the living room and I said to me husband, 'She's not stopping here. I don't want our Geoffrey hearing her'. She was behind me, and she heard. She put her hands on my shoulders and she said, 'That's the way we are in London, chick. I won't swear again while I'm here'.

(M.W.)

## The Pie Man

When I started work I worked for Andrews, a confectioner in Ashton – Market Avenue it was. My job was cleaning tins and wheeling pies and things down from the bakehouse, which was on Cork Street, just behind Penny Meadow, to the shop. Andrews' pies were in great demand in those days; they reckoned they made the best pies in Ashton. You had to get them down for half past ten, quarter to eleven, first lot of pies out; and it was continual, up and down, taking them down to the shop. Strange as it may seem, my pay at Andrews was less than what I got for taking papers. For taking papers I got 5s. I collected paper

money on a Saturday and I'd collect tips as well; the tips sometimes worked out to something like 2s 6d. When I was working at Andrews my pay was 5s and no tips, no anything.

(D.J.)

## A Job in T'Mill

I went to Oldham's Battery works in Denton for a few months, but I didn't like it. I had to cut something with a razor blade and I cut my fingers. Putting viscous caps on plugs – that was the job. You put them on and had to put them in the oven and bake them; then you must have had to cut something off. I can't remember properly, but I never liked that. That's why I went in the mill. I went in the doubling room at first. I didn't have a machine; I was only helping, what they call 'doffing'. When the bobbins were full I helped to take them off and put an empty one on. I did that for quite a bit. Then I went in the winding room. You have 'cops' from the spinners. The spinners get it from the card room and they spin it finer. Then we put two together; we put them on a bobbin – like a bobbin of cotton – and you had to have a machine to tie knots with, y'know weaver's knots, to make them flat. I did that for a while. I went in another room, but it gave me a bad chest. I asked to be moved, so I went back in the winding room. I went to the 'beaming'. They put loads of bobbins on a frame and do them all together. It's before the weaving. I worked 7.00a.m. to 5.30p.m. at first, but during the war we worked shifts, 6.00 till 2.00 and 2.00 till 10.00. During the war they did parachutes and things like that. I got 9s 2d to start with; that was before I went on a machine. When you got on a machine you were on piecework. That was 29s.

(D.S.)

## Finding the Right Job

My friend, Connie, got a job in the market, on the cosmetic stall. I wanted a job to be near her. So I started on the hardware in the market. It's still there; it was called Moss' then, but I think it's Bailey's now. I didn't work there very long because the wages weren't very much – about 60d a week. Somebody else in our street worked at John Hills and I thought, 'Well, better money than I get'. So I applied and got a job there. But I didn't stop very long because the heat didn't suit me. I went to Roebuck's, on Stamford Street. Then I went to Kenyon's in Dukinfield, and from there to the Empire Cinema. Later Mrs Norton, who worked at the Co-op, knew me and asked me would I go to the Co-op at the top of Stamford Street as a cleaner, for three days a week. Then I started in the shop and I were there twenty years. I retired at fifty-nine.

(A.A.)

## The Confectioner's Shop

Went to work in a confectioner's on Oldham Road, where the traffic lights are, at Wilshaw Lane there. There's the public house on the corner and the row of houses went back. It was a confectioner's there. I stayed there a couple of years, and then I moved to another confectioner's, nearer home, in Egerton Street. The confectioner's was called Matley's. I used to have to grease the tins and they didn't roll the pastry out for the little meat pies. You just put a roll of pastry in the tin and you put it in a machine and pressed and it presses it out. In our lunch break we used to have a walk round, round Lordsfield, and those houses weren't there then. They were all allotments and hen pens and things like that.

(A.B.)

## Down at the Jam Factory

I went to work at Robertson's; it was only in the warehouse, packing jars of jam. We used to go picking strawberries. That was a horrible job; I used to come home black and used to have to use bleach on my hands. Sometimes, on dry fruit – currants and raisins – y'know how sometimes it sticks together, we had to go and sort that out, if they thought we'd not enough work on the warehouse side.

(Mrs E.C.)

## Butcher's Boy

I went into the butcher's down Oldham Road, facing Christchurch. I were errand boy-cum-training; I were boning out and taking orders and serving when I weren't out on the bike. Every butcher had errand boys in them days; some had two or three. It were all done by bike. [There was] one customer up near t' barracks. Just imagine, I'm going from here on a heavy bike; it's pouring with rain. And then wintertime were wintertime, not like it is today; they don't know what snow is, or ice. This butcher's brother-in-law, a police sergeant in Ashton, he resided up there. Many a time I've gone up. I've said, 'Mr Davies, I haven't got nothing written down for so and so'. 'Well', he says, 'give 'em half a pound of steak and a slice of liver with it, and take it up on spec'. On spec, up there on spec! I've gone and there's been nobody in and I've had to come back with it. I used to earn 7s 6d a week. You had a few pence knocked off anything you bought at the butchers.

(N.B.)

## The Mouse in the Paint

I became a painter's apprentice. They mixed everything, hand-mixed. I used to mix paint; all we got were gloss paints and some enamels; everything else, undercoats, primers, everything was mixed from paste paint with linseed oil. The quality of a painter was his ability to mix stuff that lasted. [Where we mixed the paint] there were mice and everything, jumping into the paint cans. They used to drown themselves. We used to put all the bits of paint together and call it 'sludge'. It came out sort of brown, and it used to be used for painting inside gutters and the first coating of the backs of old property. Of course, we often would find the tail and the remains of a mouse in it.

(J.M.)

## Decorator's Apprentice

I worked for Samuel Corlett, as a painter and decorator, from fourteen. We didn't have cars, y'know. We pushed handcarts. If you got a lad an apprentice now, he wouldn't push a handcart from here to Belle Vue or

t'Oldham or to Mottram even, with all the tackle on. I had to go to night school three nights a week after work, but that didn't do us any harm.

(B.N.)

## Knowing One's Worth

I went to Lowburn College to learn about accountancy. I remember one Friday morning I were looking at the *Reporter*, at the 'Vacancies' column and they wanted somebody in the accounts department at Manchester Corporation. I applied for it. It was advertised then at £500, which was quite a bit of money then. I got an interview with the accountant. He said, 'Right, you can have the job at £490'. I says, 'Oh, no! I don't want it at £490; I want it at £500'. I walked out and left him. About a week later I got a letter. 'Are you still interested in the job? If you are, will you give the accountant a ring?' I rung him. 'When can you start?' I got the job and they gave it me at £510, which was £10 more than it was originally. I stayed there then until I retired. The accountant said to me one day, 'I look upon you as one of my better appointments'.

(F.H.)

## Going Round the Bend

When I first started work, I worked at ICI at Blackley. I trained to be a shorthand typist. There were about five or six of us from this area who used to go. We used to go on bikes – nearly eight miles from my garden gate to going through the gates at Blackley. We used to go along the canal bank from the top of

*An aerial view of Hurst Mills. St John's church can be seen at the bottom of the picture and Queen's Road crosses the picture from left to right.*

Daisy Nook. We used to get on the canal bank there because it saved you riding up the hill on the other side. You came out at Crime Lake and when you got to Crime Lake you had to carry your bike up the steps. The weather was very different then, because we had these foggy, very foggy days. One foggy day we were riding along the canal, five of us. The canal bent round to the left. Four of us went round the bend; one drove straight on,

into the canal. We had to fish him out. He had to go home and get dried out.

(H.F.)

## Hurst Mills

There were Hurst Mills, New Mill and Carr's. There were three mills, all up at

Hurst. Me mother worked at a mill behind there called Topping's Factory, and she took me there. She learnt me a bit, and then they closed, and she got on at Hurst mills. She took me, and I were doing all right. I could pick anything up. This lady called Ellen, she learned me. It should have took six months and I was on a reel of me own in three. Reeling, did you ever see reeling? It's the quietest and cleanest beside winding in all t'mill. Where I went, at Hurst mills, they did everything, from the raw cotton to the cloth.

(E.M.)

## The Weaving Shed

I'd always fancied going in the mill, so I was thrilled to bits when I went in this weaving shed and learned weaving. It were Den Mill, off Manchester Road, Mossley. I had four looms. Me week's wages were two shillings. Me mother used to give me a shilling back for spending money. I worked damned hard. You daren't go home with less that two – you hadn't been doing your job proper if you did.

(M.W.)

## No Catholics Need Apply

It closed, that little mill where me mother worked. At different works they had an office outside where you went to inquire about jobs. D'you know what it used to say in t'window – 'No Catholics need apply'. I can see it now, as though it were yesterday.

(E.M.)

## Radcliffe's the Confectioner

When I was fourteen I went right into confectionery – Radcliffe's on Stamford Street. We had a terribly hard taskmaster. She was a biddy. If you had a hair showing under your cap, you got pulled over the coals. You daren't talk, or sing. You hadn't to talk among yourselves. We did do, but when we got word she was coming – 'She's coming; she's coming' – we just shut up. She was very bad, but she taught me a lot. They were well known, Radcliffe's cakes. You got a small loaf for 2d, and a large loaf was 5d. You could get vanillas for about 2d, eclairs 2d. You could fill a bag for 5s. I worked there till I was married in 1936. I earned 2s 6d a week. In those days you were lucky to get a place like Radcliffe's. You had to pay a premium. I graduated to 5s when I'd been there four or five years. The washing was terrible. The aprons, once you got them in water, it was just like sludge; y'had to slide it off. My mother wouldn't touch it. I had to do my own washing and clean my own bedroom.

(A.G.)

## The Biscuit-Maker

I left school when I was fourteen. I went straight from school to John Hill's biscuit factory. I worked from eight o'clock to noon and from one o'clock to five thirty each day and for that I earned 10s a week. I wrapped biscuits, packed biscuits into big tins and put cream-crackers into packets. I also creamed biscuits, which involved putting cream onto one biscuit and then putting another biscuit on top. Also I used to put stars, little gems, on biscuits. My room was Number 4 Room,

*A van bearing the logo for John Hill's biscuits.*

and the supervisors were Amy Old and Edith Davies.

(I.H.)

## Mattie the Marshmallower

When I worked at John Hill's, I helped to make marshmallows. I had a bag like the one you use for icing cakes. The marshmallow mixture had to be put into this bag and then I'd go along squeezing the marshmallow mixture onto the biscuits as quickly as I could. There were seventy-two biscuits on a board and I got a farthing (a quarter of a penny) for each board I completed. The supervisor of our room, Room 5, was a Miss Daniels, and she had to interview you before you got a job there.

(M.L.)

## The Brush Maker

I went to be an apprentice at a brush shop. There were two brothers, just over Turner Lane, Brushes and Brushes Ltd. I were learning the trade of being a brush maker. I started six o'clock in the morning and I worked for nothing for about six months because I were apprenticed. They give me my first brush, and it were when First World War were on. I made an officer's hairbrush; I'll say it myself, it were beautiful. I were going leaps and bounds and doing well there. Then I pricked a fingernail with wire, down the wick and it venomed. They wouldn't accept it, and me father took me away. 'A firm that won't accept an accident isn't worth working for', he said.

(E.M.)

## Life in the Bakery

I started in a bakery at Guide Bridge. I worked there for three years and then I went to Droylsden. After that I went to Hurst Cross, then to Cowhill Lane, then Stamford Square. Then I ended up in the bakery at Hurst Cross, the same one as before but owned by different people. It was the only thing I was interested in doing. I was leaving school at Easter and me mother took me and this man said I could have a job at Easter when I left school. The bakeries I worked in were always small places. They were usually owned by a family. I worked in the bakery, mixing bread and pastry and doing the pies and things like that. It was always a nice atmosphere. You didn't get the holidays everybody else did. I didn't go in the Whit Walks for years because I always worked on

*An advertisement for John Hill's biscuits.*

*The 'Marshmallow Girls' of John Hill's Biscuits relaxing. Mattie Kenworthy (Mrs Mattie Lee) is on the front row, far right.*

Whit Friday. I think at first I started at 5.45a.m., but in a lot of places I started at 5.30a.m.. Around Christmas you worked all night. You'd just go home, when you'd finished, for a couple of hours. At first, when I started, you got a half-day in the week and you worked Saturday morning. But you started at 5.00a.m. and till 12.30p.m. or 1.00 was as long as a normal day. You finished when you'd finished. You never got paid any extra for extra hours. When I worked in Droylsden there were no buses on Good Fridays and Whit Fridays. I'd sleep at somebody's house. I didn't even get home at all then. Easter was so busy. And New Year was like another Christmas. You only got Christmas Day and Boxing Day [off] and then you were back. You had Christmas all over again, because people had parties – they didn't go out for meals like they do now – everybody had parties at home. Then Easter, with hot-cross buns. We used to make that many. We used to have a load coming off every hour and they never got off the metal trays and got packed. They were put right into bags and sold. People were waiting for your next lot coming out. At Christmas people bought bread like there were no tomorrow. They'd be buying eight or ten large loaves. There were no freezers, like they have now; they'd just put it in t' bread bin and hope for the best.

(G.W.)

## In a Hat Shop on Union Road

My mother got work at a hat shop, on Union Road, where they made felt hats. You could buy a hat for 6d. They used to clean this felt with petrol. Well, us house was stinking through every night. Me mother used to have to take her clothes off and hang 'em in yard. Me father used to say, 'Kit, if ever I get fed up with thee, I only need to put a light to thee. Thou'll be no trouble to me'.

(E.M.)

## A Handbag for a Queen

My mother took me to the Labour Exchange. They'd opened a handbag factory in Oldham. So I went for an interview. I stopped there – it was run by the Germans –

*Nellie Schofield, Grace Wardle and Edna Godfrey outside Hall's Bakery, Droylsden.*

well into the war. I finished up making samples. I made a handbag for Queen Mary, but they weren't allowed the coat of arms because they were Germans. She ordered a handbag at the International Trade Fair, and she'd sent the material.

(M.B.)

## Fred Thornley, Accountant

I left school when I was fifteen. I went to work for an accountant, Fred Thornley of Ashton, on Old Street. His office was above Fish', opposite what was in those days the Majestic. I was an audit clerk. When the war started they wanted clerks on the railway. So I got a job as a booking clerk at Droylsden. From there I went to be booking clerk at Stalybridge.

(H.K.)

## The Old Woman Who Looked After the Fire

At the bakery we used to have an old woman – I mean, she was still doing it when she was eighty-odd – who came all day Sunday. She'd got that old she didn't want to keep coming and going back. She'd light the oven, 'cos it was let out a bit Saturday night, so she could clean the firebox out. She'd get it going and get the fire up and cut the potatoes up for the day after, do upstairs and do a bit of cleaning. I think he used to buy her a couple of bottles of Guinness for all day Sunday – eight o'clock till about 6.00p.m.

(G.W.)

Queen Mary on the steps of Ashton Town Hall.

## The Price of King Cotton

This day I'm going down for some water; it were a very hot day. I had to pass by where there were the cotton chamber. I saw a crowd. I'll never forget it. They got this young man out. He'd got fast. It had clicked and clicked and locked him in. If I never stir again, he stood, they held him, and d'you know what I saw? Everything black; burnt to a cinder! I didn't know whether to faint, throw cup down or run home. I stood with my mouth open, and I said, 'Oh, glory be to God'. Manager came to me and he says, 'Where are you from, lassie?' I said 'Reeling Room'. He says, 'Go home'. 'I mustn't do

*National Gas and Oil cricket team. Mr Tom Lee is on the extreme right on the front row.*

that', I said. 'I must go back to my work'. I don't think that young feller (he'd be six foot; he were only in his twenties), I don't think he'd get above £1 or twenty-five shillings a week.

(E.M.)

## Working Women in Wartime

I transferred from Crossley Brothers, on Pottery Lane in Manchester (to which I had walked every day from Mansfield Street in Ashton), to the National in Ashton. I had learned grinding, milling and drilling at Crossley Brothers. I told the National that I was a miller. They had no machine to put me on. So Tommy Hulme, the manager, put me on a surface grinder; it was the only one in the works. I met Tom, my husband, when I borrowed his 0-1 micrometer. Later on, because I could read a micrometer, I inspected jobs, and I even got to inspect Tom's work. I worked from eight o'clock to five o'clock each day, and the money was good. I worked there until I had to give up work to look after mum.

(M.L.)

## Starting Pay

My mother took me down for an interview with the personnel manager at the

National. Me background was excellent, of course, with going to the Tech., you see! I got a job at the National. I started work in April 1948, in the drawing office, as the errand boy. I had to run about with all the drawings and everything ; as they printed the drawings, you'd take them to the different offices. I started work there at the enormous sum of 18s (90p) a week. The lads in the works, the apprentices, were on 32s (£1.60) a week. I had to spend three months in the drawing office before I could go into the works and get the big money, 32s a week. My mother used to give me 5s (25p) a week spending money out of that 18s a week.

(J.E.)

## Do You Know What You're Doing?

I went to work at a station, Miles Platting, which was then a very big station, in September 1948. A chap put a lot of paper in front of me, all these columns, and he said, 'Add them up'. I added the columns up. I had to balance them; nothing balanced across the bottom at all. It got to dinnertime and he looked over his shoulder and didn't seem very happy. In the afternoon he decided to have a look at these lists of figures of mine. 'Do you know what you're doing?' 'Well', I said, 'I'm adding them up in tons, hundredweights, quarters and pounds'. 'Well', he said 'they're pounds, shillings and pence'. This is a payroll office. Nobody had told me, nobody!

(A.B.)

## I'm Bored

I worked in the draughtsman's office, which was totally wrong for me. I used to take the blueprints around to various sections of the firm and I used to be fascinated with watching the people using their hands. One day I went to the chief of the department and said, 'Look, I'm bored. I want to go in the works'. 'You what!', he said. 'What do you want to do?' 'I want to be an engineer'. A week after, he said, 'Are you still of the same mind?' 'Yes', I said. 'Right, you can go in the works. Start on Monday'. Came home, said to mother, 'Will you buy me some overalls?'. 'Overalls! What for?' 'I'm going in the works'. She bounced me off every wall in the kitchen because to have a white-collar job, y'know, [that was the thing].

(H.C.)

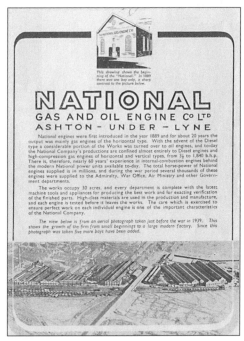

An advertisement for National Gas and Oil Engine Co.

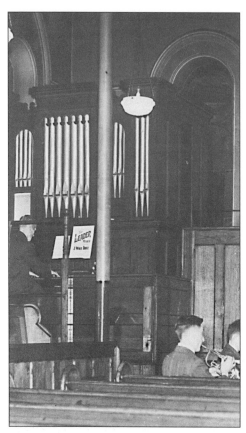

*The organ at Henry Square Methodist church.*

## Careers Advice! What Careers Advice?

They brought a careers advisor around school – I don't think they called them that in those days. She said, 'We'll have to find something special for you. Would you like to do gardening in Stamford Park, or would you like to be an organ builder, church organs?' I knew what gardening was like and I had no inclination to be a gardener. I had no idea what making church organs amounted to. I said I wanted to be an electrician or something like that. I got no more help from school or the education system in choosing a job. After I left school

I put my best suit on one day and I walked towards Manchester, down Ashton Old Road, calling in all the electrical firms and the like on the way down until eventually I found one that showed interest in me. Later that night they sent a message asking me to go down for an interview with the boss of the firm and I started a seven-year apprenticeship. All I did to get a job was to walk down the road until I found someone who would take me on.

(H.I.)

## A Foggy Day in Ashton Town

I remember me uncle walking from work one night, when we lived on the Moss, and he was so late we were absolutely worried sick. The fog was so thick he'd been wandering for hours, just going round in circles; he'd got down on that part of the Moss where there's all market gardens. He just didn't know where he was. When it was foggy it used to be all over your hair; you could put your hand on your hair and it was pitch black. You just couldn't see your hand in front of you.

When I worked in Droylsden, for Stuart Hall, who's on TV now, and we lived over the Moss, I always remember finishing work and there were no buses running because of the fog. A lad came in with a scooter and Stuart Hall paid him to go in front of us, because he could see a bit better. When we got to Chester Square, he said, 'I'm not taking you over the Moss; I'll be all night'. I remember going along the wallside, and it took me hours to get home, holding onto the wall. I thought, 'Well, that's the end of the wall. If I walk straight, I'll come to the next corner'. By the time Stuart Hall got to

Stalybridge the fog had disappeared. He actually got home to Glossop a lot quicker than I did. It was so frightening.

(G.W.)

## The Trams

Trams ran from Manchester to Ashton. They came along Old Street; then, when they were going back, they went along Stamford Street. So there were tramlines in the road. I remember I was allowed to stay up once because there was a tram which was supposed to have come all the way from Liverpool. The tramlines were connected, they said, and you could come all the way from Liverpool to Ashton. Trams were sometimes illuminated, perhaps for a trade show or something. The trams were double-deckers. They had a door at the front and at the back. There was always a conductor on them. Certain trams, only certain ones, had seats that could be moved.

(H.K.)

## Ashton's Stations

At Ashton Wakes everything used to close. There'd be a very big fair on the market, but, if you wanted to buy anything, you had to move out. Lots of people went off to Blackpool. Ashton had stations then.

*A double-decker tram outside Ashton Town Hall, c. 1910.*

Charlestown station was always busy. We had Oldham Road Station, just the other side of where the bridge is on Oldham Road. There was also Park Bridge station. A friend of mine, who was rejected for the army on health grounds, was stationmaster at Park Parade. I always saw him when I came home on leave. He'd say to me, 'David, we'll have a couple of hours out. I'll shut up'. Then he used to shut the station down. Only about two trains a day came through, but somebody had to be there.

(D.J.)

## Fighting to Get On

One of the best things of going to Ashton was that the railway stations were interesting; there were always a few good trains to see. Particularly at holiday times the stations in Ashton would get packed. I remember going on holiday and getting the train from Ashton Charlestown station – an excursion train – and standing back while the doors opened and literally fighting to get on.

(A.B.)

## The Old Lady Who Knew

We went to live at 197 Curzon Road. In that row lived a Mrs Smith, a very handy lady at that time. Had anybody died, first person they'd [the family] go for was Mrs Smith. Three half crowns (about 38p now) and she'd get the body ready, washed, all done up. She'd been doing it all her life, and she was well in her seventies.

*A Manchester tram in Bow Street, c. 1910. The tram outside the Town Hall is an Ashton tram.*

There was a row of houses at the back of ours; they just ended and there was a big piece of spare ground. This buldozer came and started to bulldoze the spare ground. When I got home from work at the Co-op shoe-repairer's at Hurst Cross, Mrs Smith came and knocked on door. 'Don't you mind just coming out back here?' she says. I went out and she said, ;Have you looked at yon gable end?' 'What?', I said. 'Gable end of yon row'. 'No, I've never looked at it'. 'Well', she says, 'have a look'. There were two window sills and a door in the middle, and two smaller windows over the top. They were all bricked up. Mrs Smith says, 'Can we walk over there?' She walked to her house and said, 'I live there, and I were born there. I used to come to work with me dad. He walked out of the house here and he walked over to that window in the gable end. See that window. It's only low. Glass opened, didn't it? That were lamp room for pit, yon window there and t'other were th'office. I'd walk with dad here, and sometimes he'd let me hand in his tally – his number – and then they'd give him his lamp. That were the only way they knew whether he were down pit or not. Then he'd walk here (almost level with their door) and that were it. He'd give me a kiss and he got in the cage'. Then she says, 'Now then, are they going to put owt there? If he comes with yon thing [the bulldozer], he'll go straight down, and it were a right deep pit'. Following day I went down to Town Hall. Told them what had happened and that the old lady were worried sick. They didn't believe me, but next day someone did come from Town Hall. I took him to Mrs Smith and said, 'Now lass, tell him what you told me'. She did. For a while work stopped on the site. Then building began. It was quickly abandoned and lorries began to arrive from all over bringing stuff to fill in the pit. Y'have to listen to old people. They have a tale to tell.

(F.R.)

# CHAPTER 7

# Entertainment and Leisure

*Old Street. The Pavilion can be seen in the distance, the tallest building on the left.*

## Cinema: Silent Movies

There was the Queen's, at the bottom of Henrietta Street. Then there was the Star, on Church Street. There was the Pavilion, and then there was the Empire, and the Theatre Royal, which was across the way [from the Empire]. Somebody used to play the piano. I remember a Scottish film and my sister-in-law was singing and my father-in-law was playing the bagpipes. I don't know if it was *Rob Roy*. The seats weren't comfortable, like they are now. The front row were just bare boards, wooden seats; sometimes there might have been a bit of carpet on. I think it was about 3d and if you sat in the back stalls it was only 6d. There was a manager who kept the boys in order. Sometimes they'd be so noisy they'd be tipped out.

(Mrs A.B.)

## The Ryecroft Cinema

We used to go to a cinema in Ryecroft, on William Street. There used to be one called 'The Bunnydrome'. Before it was the Bunnydrome, it was John Hill's biscuit place, and we never called it the Bunnydrome, we called it John Hill's. We used to go there Saturday morning when we were kids, and they used to have an impromptu variety thing. Any kid that could do anything used to go up on the stage. It was run by a gentleman called Mr Power; he had a wooden leg. You used to get a prize if you came out on top. But woe betide you if you dropped your orange, because it went right down to the front. It sloped like that, you see. If you dropped anything, you had to retrieve it at the end.

(A.G.)

## 'The Bunny'

They had a cinema on Stockport Road. It was called 'The Bunny'. We used to go there on a Saturday morning. I think it was either a penny or tuppence. They used to have a piano. If you made too much noise, they stopped the film and put the lights up till you quietened down. They had things like the serials, Tom Mix and Flash Gordon. It must have been very dangerous really. There was only a very narrow staircase to go up.

(D.S.)

## Let this Girl Sit Down

Me mother used to take us to the Queen's on a Friday night; it was a lot cheaper than the Majestic. There was another one when we lived down Stockport Road – the Bunnydrome they called that. When you went on a Saturday afternoon you couldn't get a seat. I had a great big doll and I took this one Saturday afternoon. The manager came in and he said to somebody, 'Why don't you get up and let this girl sit down carrying a child?' Two lads got up, while I sat down. He didn't know it were a doll. The manager used to march round and keep all the children quiet. It were only 1d, that's all. If we got a Saturday penny, we took it to the Bunnydrome.

(M.W.)

## Reading the Subtitles

When the cinema was silent, she (my sister) used to read the titles to me. I used to say, 'What does it say?' and she'd read it to me.

(M.B.)

## The Pavilion

As we grew up we started going to the Pavilion, in Old Street. Turns used to come on there at the interval, y'know, on the stage. There used to be a picture and then there would be a turn. Sometimes it would be a singer. They were silent films, and there would be a pianist. It were nice.

(E.M.)

## The Queen's

We used to go to the Queen's. I remember going with some relatives from Yorkshire.

*In this picture of the Whit Walks, c. 1935, the Queen's cinema, showing the latest Bing Crosby film, can be seen in the background.*

We went downstairs and we went in the side entrance. We were on the front row, looking like that [sideways] at the picture. We sat on wooden forms. You were posh if you went upstairs. Odd times you used to go to Queen's for the first house and the Pavilion for the second house, or the Majestic.

(E.C.)

## Showing Pictures in Stages

I were friendly with a girl; her father was a decorator and they had a wallpaper shop the far end of Old Street, near the war memorial. Three of us used to go to the Pavilion, upstairs – it was only 9d. I went to the Queen's once or twice. I didn't like it, although the music was all right. When the cowboys were coming, she'd be banging away on the piano. They used to show pictures in stages; you'd see one part one week, and the next the next week. You'd be going mad if you missed one part.

(Mrs E.C.)

## Sweeney Todd

The Queen's was a small cinema. I remember seeing Tod Slaughter in *Sweeney Todd* or *Murder at the Red Barn*, all black and white and sometimes silent. You went up some steps to the Queen's; it was built on a slope.

(J.M.)

## If You Were Broke

More often than not we went to the Empire or the Pavilion. Sometimes we went to the

Queen's; that wasn't such a nice cinema. It had a little balcony; it also had a much cheaper admission charge. I don't think it showed a film that wasn't thirty-years old, and a good many of them were silent films. It was brightly painted inside. In fact, they used to change the paintwork fairly often; I think they did it themselves. The seats weren't comfortable. It just didn't seem as sophisticated – if that's the word – as the others. You went to the Queen's if you couldn't get in anywhere else, or if you were broke.

(A.B. and E.B.)

## A Bit Rough

We went to nearly all the cinemas in Ashton. We used to go to the Queen's; it was a bit rough there, so you didn't go there too often. When I was working, I was once taking a break with the bricklayer and the labourer, and we were talking about the films. 'Who's at the Queen's?' Randolph Scott were there; he were always there. The bricklayer says, 'He were there that many times during the war, Randolph Scott, he must have had digs around the corner'.

(B.P.)

## Horror Film

I remember looking in the *Reporter* to see what was on and there was something on at the Queen's which was a nice thing. So this friend and I went and what I'd been looking at was not what was on that week, but the week after. We saw a horrible film called *The Terror*. All I can remember of it – I had my

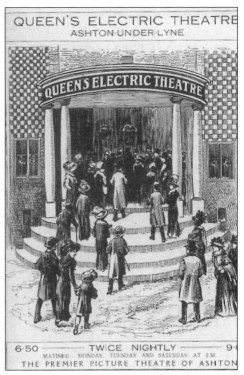

A drawing of entrance to Queen's Electric Theatre, c. 1913.

face covered most of the time – was somebody down in the cellar playing an organ. It was awful!

(I.S.)

## The Empire

I worked at the Empire; I was usherette downstairs mainly. I did go in the pay – box for a little while. I don't say I were very clever at reckoning up. [Tickets] were 1s 9d and 2s 6d when I were there. I remember Mr Robinson, the manager; when there was a film with Frank Sinatra, he stood at the back. He'd come down from his office and watch it at nearly every performance. There

The Empire Hippodrome.

A programme for The Messiah at the Empire.

An advertisement for the Majestic cinema, now
the Metro, c. 1939.

was an organ; there was always an organ
recital. It used to come up out of the floor.
You could make requests. 'We'll gather
lilacs' was one of my requests. Me friend that
worked there, she had 'Because'. They also
had all the shows there, the operatic shows.

(A.A.)

## The Majestic/The Gaumont

People used to go to the pictures in family
groups, didn't they? I remember me aunty
taking us to the Majestic, half a row of us, to
see *Snow White and the Seven Dwarfs*. There
were probably about ten of us and a couple
of aunties, one at each end. 'Now, behave
yourself'. I remember going there to see the
Errol Flynn film about Robin Hood.

(A.B.)

## Projectionist at the Gaumont

I had an aunt who was a projectionist at the Gaumont. I remember seeing *Dumbo* there for free. She took me up in the projection box while they were showing *Dumbo* in the early 1940s.

(J.E.)

## He Was Late

If it was cricket season Alan used to say, 'I'll meet you inside'. More often than not we went to the Empire or the Pavilion, because you could book in advance. He'd give me the ticket and then meet me inside. If he was late, I lost my temper; but I always waited for him. The Gaumont particularly had a long waiting room upstairs, with chairs in it. I used to sit in there.

(E.B.)

## Tickets on the Back Row

I remember going to the Gaumont, sitting on the front row, when I was a kid; it was only about 9d then, on the front row. Then, when I was getting in my teens, I started taking the girls on the back row of the 1s 9d upstairs.

(J.E.)

## The Star on Church Street

We used to go to the Star Picture House on Church Street. It was the biggest rat-hole you could find. They called it 'The Bug House'. If there had ever been a fire there, it would have been 'The Lord help everybody'. It was a death trap.

(A.G. and M.B.)

## The Woman to the Box Office was Drunk

The Star was on Church Street, where the GPO sorting office is now. We used to say that, if you waited till later on in the week, it was easy to get in, because the woman who worked in the box-office was drunk.

(H.K.)

*The Star cinema.*

**★ STAR CINEMA - First & Best ★**

CHURCH ST., ASHTON, Manager: Geo. Lowe. Tel Ash. 1124

| NOV. 7th—MON., TUES., WED.: | THURSDAY, FRIDAY SATURDAY— |
| DONALD COOK in— | RICHARD DIX in "THE |
| "CIRCUS GIRL" | DEVIL IS DRIVING |
| Also GENE AUTRY in— | Also KEN MAYNARD in— |
| GUNS AND GUITARS | HEROES of the RANGE |

MATINEES: Mon., Tues., and Thurs., 2d. and 3d. Saturday Matinee, 1d. and 2d.

*An advertisement for the Star cinema in the 1940s.*

## The Bug Hut

The Star was like 'The Bug Hut'. The film was always breaking down. The Star was a lot cheaper than the other cinemas. You walked right up Church Street; it was where the post office is now. Even when we were young we could go, 'cos you only had to turn at our corner, walk past Harry Iliffe's house and the yard where his dad made the ice cream. Sometimes there was a film on that carried on from week to week. When we were very young, me dad used to take us – I can't remember whether it were on Wednesday or Thursday – to see something.

*(G.W.)*

## It Rained In

I did go to the Star; I've been to the Star with Harry Iliffe before now. That was a ruin of a place. If it rained, y'had to find a drier spot, quite literally. Oh, yes! I've felt the rain on me head many a time in the Star. But it was cheap and they didn't ask any questions about your age. If you thought it was going to be an exciting film

they were glad of your custom. They used to call it 'The Bug' – you very often came out with something you hadn't taken in with you.

*(A.B.)*

## A Tuppenny and a Hammer

The Star cinema was known as the Bug Hut. When you went to the paybox, which was small – like a telephone box – you'd ask the woman for 'a tuppenny and a hammer please' (the hammer being to kill the bugs). Then you had to be careful, because you had to go past the door of the pay-box to get into the picture house and she sometimes popped out and clouted you one.

*(H.I.)*

## The Ranch

There was one cinema I never went to, on Church Street, called the Star. We used to call it the Ranch; you got full of arrows and that when you went in there. The first three rows used to be covered in horse muck, they

116

said, and arrows used to be stuck in the seats. They showed that many westerns.

(J.E.)

## 'I'm Not Going Again'

Mother and dad used to take us to the Star on Church Street one night in the week. They used to have a serial – *Flash Gordon* – so we used to go one night every week and follow the serial. Then, one week, the cowboy with the white hat got killed and I cried, and me dad said, 'I'm not going again'. That was the end of that.

(J.I.)

## Children's Cinema Club

As we got old enough to go to the pictures by ourselves we used to go to the Odeon at Guide Bridge to the Childrens' Cinema Club. They used to show films specially for you and then they put music up on the screen and we used to sing to it. If you became a member of the club, you always got a card for your birthday. If you took that card with you, you and a friend could get in free that week.

(J.I.)

## The Odeon, Guide Bridge

As you got older you used to go to the

*The Odeon at Guide Bridge, c. 1936. The Mill on the Floss is playing today,* The Outcast *from Monday next. Note Commissionaire and the advertisement for* The Mickey Mouse Club.

Saturday Morning Club at the cinema. We went to the Odeon Guide Bridge. It used to be absolutely full, and it was deafening. Later we used to go on a Saturday night, and you had to queue so long to get in. Many a time we've gone for the first house and queued right through and gone in the second house because it's been so full. Then, if there were eight or ten of us, we had to split up, even so, to get in.

(G.W.)

## Saturday Afternoons

Then, of course, there was the Odeon at Guide Bridge. This is the one I used to go to a lot as a kiddie, on Saturday afternoons. Flash Gordon, Buck Rogers, Johnny Mack Brown, you name 'em, they were all there. When we were coming out, if we'd been watching Flash Gordon or Buck Rogers, we all had our ray guns, y'know. If it was a western, blasting away at each other on the way home, slapping our backsides, pretending they were horses, all the way down the road.

(J.E.)

## State of the Art

They demolished a mill to build the Odeon at Guide Bridge. I remember them pulling the mill down. The Odeon was a state of the art cinema. Me dad used to take me every Friday – 4d I think it was. I remember, if there was anything particularly ugly in the Movietone News, they used to put the lights up and all the children had to come out. We were taken into the foyer and given an ice cream, until the ugly piece of news had been seen. Any

damage, or bloodshed, or entry into the prison camps, they'd put the lights on and we were all ushered out, and not allowed back inside, so we didn't see the news.

(A.B.)

## The Roxy, Hurst

Dad used to pay for me to go to the Roxy. While we were in there, Jerry came over. They kept us in, while he passed over. Everybody were frightened to death of going when 't were time to come out. I run all road from Roxy here. I didn't go again. But the Roxy never closed; they kept going.

(E.M.)

## Doing a Turn

It only cost 4d to get in the Roxy. There was no upstairs and downstairs; it was a gradual rise to the seats at the back. That cost you 1s, to get in the seats at the back. If you went in the 1s seats, you were posh. The doors at the front were quite wide doors. Just inside was reception, where you paid your money. Either side of reception were a few stairs which went up to the back of the cinema. There used to be a chap who looked after us called Tommy Bennett. He must have been a sort of commissionaire. He used to watch the kids don't get in for nothing. During the war there were artists on stage at the Roxy. Whoever thought they could do a bit of a turn would be on stage one night a week. They used to have a magic lantern show. A chap at the back of the cinema, who put the photographs on the screen, would shine the light on a chap on the stage holding a mirror. All the kids would be sat at the front, and this lad at the back would shine his light on the mirror. The chap with the mirror would pick one of the kids out with his mirror. If he picked you out, you got a prize. My wife used to go and see Esther Williams there in the films, and when she went home, she used to swim home, pretending she were Esther Williams.

(B.P.)

## Tommy the Commissionaire

Tommy Bennett, the commissionaire; he had a uniform on, with a very large hat that had a peak on – a bit like Gestapo – and he stood about 4ft 6ins in his stockinged feet. He had a club-foot. He terrorized all the kids. He used to come round with a stick. If you weren't lined up properly outside, he used to crack you on your shins, 'Move in there'. If anybody was making a noise while the film was on – which very often happened; there was a lot of barracking, specially Saturday afternoon, and throwing things - he'd come round and he'd throw them all out. He'd find them out, Tommy Bennett.

(B.N.)

## Never on the Circuit

It was just prior to the Second World War when they built the Roxy cinema. They never got on the circuit; they were always old films that had been in [central] Ashton before they got to the Roxy. A chap called Sumner was the manager; he lived on King's Road. They used to have talent competitions to get people in. Donald Peers was the celebrity at the

The Roxy cinema, Hurst, in the late 1940s. The film is The Shop at Sly Corner, which marked Diana Dors' debut in films.

opening of the Roxy. It was a nice cinema. I used to go regularly.

(H.C.)

## Stepped Seating

The Roxy was an unusual cinema. It didn't have a circle; it was stepped. You had your stalls; then, at the back of the stalls, there was an aisle, running parallel with the stalls; then you had about three steps up, and then the back stalls. Because they were slightly higher, it was like being in the circle. It was quite a big cinema. It used to change its programme half way [through the week]: you'd get one film Monday, Tuesday and

An advertisement for the Roxy in 1951.

Wednesday and a different programme Thursday, Friday and Saturday. There was a different programme on Sunday night, very often an old film.

(J.E.)

## Taking the Bottles Back

Then, of course, we had the Roxy cinema; that was the place. They changed films there three times a week. I think it was 3d or 4d to go in there. We used to take a few bottles back. When you took empty mineral bottles back to the shop, you got 1d on them. Then we'd go to the pictures with that money.

(B.N.)

## The Cinema in Wartime

The queues during the war, with the army at the barracks and the army at Whittaker's Mill, were huge. You got in a queue and if the 'Sorry: Full' sign went up, you used to dash to the next queue. There was the Majestic, the Queen's, the Empire, Theatre Royal, and then the Odeon at Guide Bridge and the Roxy at Hurst. We used to dash from one to another, or we'd get a bus, to get in at the second house. I became a messenger in the ARP, when I was sixteen; one of the other messengers was an assistant projectionist at the Roxy. We used to be allowed into the projection room, and I was fascinated by a disc he had on the wall. It was 'Knightsbridge' and I knew that, if he ever played that, it was fire and the attendants had to evacuate the cinema. I remember we stayed in the cinema at the start of the Manchester blitz. When we came out, we found that the whole sky was red and the noise and everything was quite frightening. You could see all the fires that had started in Manchester that night.

(J.M.)

## Terror in the Dark

It was a treat for me to go to the cinema. I remember me mother taking me to see *Mrs Miniver* and even me mother came out crying. When I was about fourteen Dorothy Suchabody (McGuire) was in a film called *The Spiral Staircase*. I said to me mum, 'Can I go and see it?' 'No', she says. 'You're not seeing that,' I went with Mavis Warburton, and I was petrified. I couldn't sleep; I was so afraid. So I got told off for going, 'cos she could tell immediately that I'd been to see the picture.

(E.B.)

## Meet Me Outside Henry Moon's

Henry Moon's were paper merchants. You always met your girlfriend there. 'Seven o'clock I'll be outside Henry Moon's'. You'd be stood there with your best suit on and a raincoat over your arm.

(B.N.)

## The Theatre Royal

Dad loved the theatre. It was a red-letter day when we used to go to the Palace Theatre in Manchester, which he thought was great. He loved the Theatre Royal in Ashton. He always used to go before the war. When he came home, of course, that tradition started again. Every Thursday night was theatre night. After a few years the shows weren't so much good family shows. He wouldn't take me anywhere that was a bit off. So he stopped going to the theatre.

(E.B.)

## All the Top Stars

The Theatre Royal used to have all the top stars. After the war they had a repertory company. That chap who became a film star – Ronald Fraser – he was part of the repertory company. I rather think Robert Donat was, at one time.

(H.K.)

*The Theatre Royal.*

*An advertisement for the Theatre Royal.*

*A programme for the Theatre Royal.*

## A Mouse Ran Over My Foot

While I was working at the Empire I used to get a pass for the Theatre Royal. When I'd finished at night, I'd go across to the Theatre Royal and have the last couple of hours there before I went home. But the last time I went a mouse ran over my foot, so I never went again. It was when it was getting a very old building.

(A.A.)

## Fantastic!

There was the Theatre Royal. It was a disgrace that place was pulled down, because it was an old Victorian Music Hall, with gilt boxes, gods and everything. We used to get loads of acts there, quite a lot of well-known radio comedians like Frank Randle, Harry

Corris. They had magicians, comedians, showgirls. Fantastic!

(J.E.)

## Matinees

On Saturday afternoon at the Theatre Royal they used to have film matinees for children. They used to have serials, and a lot were about Africa, the jungle drums and everything, scaring you to death.

(I.S.)

## The Palais-de-Danse

We used to go dancing at Ashton Palais. We also used to go dancing at the Premier – that was on Park Parade, I think. It was a little dance hall, a nice place to go. That's gone a long time now. Ashton Palais was a wooden building, all wood, all tarred; how it was not set on fire, I don't know. You'd go Friday night to a big band. You thought you were paying dear; it was 10s (50p) and you saw them all there. A good night it was.

(B.P.)

## Terrific Dance Band

Ashton Palais – dance hall supreme. Everybody went to Ashton Palais. They used to have all the big dance bands; one a month came there. We also had a terrific dance band in Ashton – the Ashton Palais Orchestra was a good dance band.

(B.N.)

## Change out of Sixpence

My dad remembered when the Palais opened as an ice-skating rink. I wasn't a Palais man; my wife used to go to the Palais. I used to go to a dance hall at the end of Old Street. My sisters could dance and they used to teach me at home to dance. I recollect the first time they said, 'Right, you're coming with us'. And we went to the Palais. In those days they used to have 'Excuse-me' dances. I'd been sat there and me youngest sister said to me, 'Come on, you're getting up'. I said, 'I'm not'. She was going to tell my mother if I didn't get up. So I got up. I also went to Waterloo Liberal Club. I was on the staff there. I don't think I was an awfully good dancer, but, at least, I could teach others what to do. When I went to Waterloo Liberal Club, I used to go out with sixpence (2p); it was tuppence to go into the dance; it was tuppence halfpenny for a jug of beer in the Woodman opposite, and I had change out of sixpence. That was just prior to the war.

(H.C.)

## Watching the Dancers

We started going to the Palais on a Monday night. None of us could dance, not ballroom dancing. We were only sixteen. It was 1s 6d to go in the balcony and watch the dancers, also the band. It was an excellent band – a drummer, a pianist (the pianist was Raymond Woodhead, who had a choir on BBC radio for a good number of years), a guy on the double bass, three trombones, three trumpets, five saxes. One of the saxes used to double up on the clarinet for the Dixieland numbers. They used to play a lot of the Stan Kenton stuff, and

# PALAIS-de-DANSE

## ASHTON-under-LYNE

★ The Most Popular Ballroom in the District with the Resident Broadcasting Band ... playing at all sessions

PRIVATE DANCING LESSONS
BY APPOINTMENT

★

*Modern Dancing*
MONDAY, TUESDAY
FRIDAY, SATURDAY

★

*Olde Tyme Dancing*
THURSDAY

☆

*Glider Skating*
WEDNESDAY

★

General Manager : S. G. ROBERTS
Tel.: ASHTON 1896

**TO DANCE ORGANISERS**—The Ballroom is available on Tuesday and Friday evenings for Private and Semi-Private Dances. Make sure that your dance is a success by booking the District's Finest Ballroom

*An advertisement for Ashton Palais.*

*Ashton Palais Tramways' dance, 1932.*

a lot of the be-bop numbers of the era, Ted Heath and all this sort of thing. It was a damn good 1s 6d worth just to watch them and listen to this band playing. We used to get bands like Ted Heath, Geraldo, Vic Lewis, Teddy Foster, Oscar Rabin; all the big bands used to come to the Palais. The resident band was the Raymond Woodhead Orchestra, though we used to call it the Palais Band. I saw Dickie Valentine and Cleo Laine there, when they were young. It was 1s 6d; they used to put it up to 2s 6d when the big bands were there. The Palais was a timber building; it was a fire hazard. I'm surprised it never went up in smoke, because everybody smoked in those days. When you got on the dance floor, you couldn't just dance wherever you wanted When you got on that floor, the whole lot moved round. The floor was completely massed. If you were doing a samba or a rumba, it wasn't so bad, because there weren't as many on the floor. If they played a be-bop number, something like 'Woodchopper's Ball', a section of the dancers, the boppers, would get round by the band. Some of those boppers were fantastic.

(J.E.)

## The Mad Hatter

The Mad Hatter was a café on Stamford Street in the 1950s. We used to have a glass of coffee; it were something different, you see. Little Lads' Beer House really it was. We used to come out of night school and go there in the interval, and then teacher comes in, 'Are you coming back to school?' The Saints' Jazz Band played in the café. They went on to play at the Festival Hall in London.

(B.N.)

*Billy Wood's 'Ohios' at Ashton Palais.*

## Getting the Skates On

I took a craze at one time for skating. It was during the war, Tuesday night at the Palais. It was roller skates. That went on for a while and then I got fed up. I think I fell a bit too much.

(E.B.)

## Eyeing the Boys

When we were girls, Stamford Street on a Sunday night was what was called 'The Monkey Run'. You came out of church and you walked up there and you were eyeing the boys. They had a band in Stamford Park. As you went in the gate, they had a canvas thing that you threw money in.

(A.G.)

THE
# W. H. Broadhead & Son

## Pantomime Cinderella Danse,

AT THE

### PALAIS DE DANSE,
**Ashton-under-Lyne,**

### Friday, April 9th, 1926.

——

DANCING FROM 8-0 p.m.
CARRIAGES 2-0 a.m.

*A programme for Pantomime Cinderella Danse at Ashton Palais.*

## The Monkey Run

Stamford Street was the place on a Sunday night. You were all dressed up in your best suit. There were five or six gangs of us. We used to walk down Stamford Street and the girls would walk up the other side. They called it 'The Monkey Run'. Then you'd go on the market ground and you'd get one or two of these fellows spouting there. Pat Johnson, a vicar at Christ Church, Oldham Road, used to come on. We were more interested in the girls.

(B.N.)

## A Den of Sin and Iniquity

I'd started dancing before the war and I used to go to places like St Anne's, Burlington Street, which was a popular one at the time. I also went to the Premiere; that was a dance hall. An aunty of mine, when she heard that I was dancing, said, 'David, I don't mind you dancing so much, although I don't agree with dancing. Promise me one thing'. 'What's that?', I said. 'Keep away from Ashton Palais. That's nothing but a den of sin and iniquity'. The Palais is where I met my wife Betty during the war.

(D.J.)

*The finale of* Brigadoon, *performed by the Ashton Operatic Society at Empire Theatre in the 1950s.*

*The gentlemen of* The Merry Widow *performed by the Ashton Operatic Society.*

*David Fletcher in* Brigadoon.

## Ashton Operatic

After I came out of the army, I was at a loose end. My mother suggested, 'Why don't you join the Operatic?' I really liked shows, and me dad had done a bit, of course, and me uncle, and they persuaded me. The Operatic's musical director was called Albert Kent; he was a wonderful pianist. You had to audition before you could get into the Operatic; so I went to an audition for singing. I'd never done anything in front of anybody in my life before. The audition was at Oxford Mill Social Club, down Guide Bridge there. I'd decided to sing *Bless this house*. There was only about five people there. Then they announced, 'Now, to sing for you, David Fletcher, nephew of the great Charles Fletcher'. Someone heard and they flocked in. It was like hundreds seemed to have

come. I was petrified, absolutely petrified. I said, 'I've got a bit of a sore throat', and I chickened out. I gave my mum a bit of stick when I got back. Anyway I thought, 'I've never chickened out of anything in my life'. So, come the next week, I thought, 'I'll have to go through with it'. And I did go through with it. Anything off the piano is worse than with a band. The piano shows every imperfection, whereas a band hides it. I started off nervous, but I got a bit better. And Albert – I could have strangled him – said, 'Second verse, please'. I got through it. I must have sweat gallons. I got a few claps. Anyhow, he said 'Accepted'. I was quite surprised. I went into *Brigadoon*, which is one of my favourite shows, an absolutely marvellous show to be in. I had a wonderful time, but they put me in the dancing, didn't they? I wondered what that signified. Later I did *The Merry Widow*, *The Dubarry*, and *The Pajama Game*, but I missed *West Side Story*.

(D.F.)